Contents

Contents

Giving Birth to the Discipline Gradient

I first started teaching parenting classes when I was pregnant with my first child. Carol Brice and I had met several years earlier in our master's program at the University of Alaska Fairbanks. Carol's emphasis in the community counseling program was parent-child relationships; mine was family therapy. Besides the immediate bond of similar interests, we shared a commitment to improve family life. In March 1984, Family Training Associates (FTA) was born.

Family Training Associates' first class was offered to three couples who were expecting their first babies; I was also starting to grow large as my own due date grew closer. (Subsequently, two out of three of those couples have taken other courses offered by FTA, and we find a special pleasure in sharing the news about our firstborn children, thirteen years old at the date of this writing.)

In hopes of clarifying the overabundance of parenting materials found in libraries and bookstores, I began to organize information for a new workshop. I found that discipline books often contradicted each other; many offered valuable insights not recognized by their competition. Something must be worthwhile about each of these major theories, I thought, since they have been around for a long time and each has strong proponents.

I studied the theories and concluded that different discipline techniques are valuable in different situations, depending on the age and personality of the child and the severity of the problem. The discipline gradient—a scale organizing techniques according to their ability to develop self-discipline—was born.

Our first official contract came in June, the month before my due date. "Effective Discipline" was the first discipline class offered through Family Training Associates, consisting of two sessions two weeks apart. It was the first time we tested the information I had organized.

The first session of the discipline training was a definite success. As we talked about the range of discipline techniques, it became clear that prevention and communication techniques were better at building self-discipline and self-esteem, but they didn't always have the ability to change behaviors quickly. This is where the behaviorist techniques came in. Behavior management could change severe or repetitive behaviors so both parents and children could relax and have room to rebuild self-esteem.

Between the first Saturday and the second Saturday of the contract—three weeks before the due date—my first child was born. My husband was drafted to stay at home with our two-week-old baby while I drove to the city of North Pole with Carol to finish teaching the last part of the contract. The confusion was amusing—no one recognized me, since I had lost thirty pounds in two weeks. An unexpected benefit resulted from my daughter's early arrival: I had to entrust this tiny life to my husband. For five hours he was solely responsible for a newborn infant, and we both learned that fathers can be just as involved in a baby's very early years, as well as later when she learns to walk, talk and play.

A whole series of classes and contracts have followed Family Training Associates' expectant beginning, and the response from the community (and statewide) has been tremendous. Today Carol Brice owns and operates the private organization, which has grown in size (there are currently seven "associates") and scope, bringing family education to individual families, childcare personnel, university students, school staff, prisons, bush families, military families, and professionals who work with families. My own family has grown as well; I now have two daughters and a son. My husband is actively involved in their growth and education.

The discipline gradient has been refined somewhat since 1984, but continues to serve Family Training Associates as a model to sort out the confusion of discipline techniques and to encourage the use of techniques which foster self-esteem and self-control in children.

We have been asked many times if there is a book that summarizes the teaching we do through Family Training Associates, especially one including information about the discipline gradient. This book is a response to that request.

I would like to salute Carol Brice, the driving force behind Family Training Associates, as a professional dedicated to encouraging families and improving the quality of family relationships. Carol's accomplishments are too numerous to mention, but everyone who knows her—or knows of her—will be quick to acknowledge her generous, never-ending support for Alaska's (and America's) families. It has been my great pleasure to work with Carol for more than fifteen years, and

I want to thank her for all her support, encouragement, expertise and friendship during the years we have worked together, with special thanks for her support of this book.

I would also like to thank all the parents and professionals who have participated in our workshops, many of whom began with our expectant-parent class and continue to return for classes on toddlers, preschoolers, school-age children, teens and other concerns. Their support and suggestions for further development have been invaluable.

I'd like to thank Carol Kaynor, Dave Partee and Renee Manfredi who have worked with me in editing this book, and friends and associates who have read chapters and offered advice and support.

I am particularly pleased to present Barbara Naki's "Cycle of Anger" in chapter 11. Barbara taught this cycle to Fairbanks professionals many years ago, and it continues to be an invaluable addition to the field of parenting education.

A special thank-you goes to my family for their encouragement and inspiration.

Introduction

The Discipline Gradient

Children are different. Parents are different. Not all discipline techniques work for all children at all times.

This book was written to organize discipline techniques so parents can choose strategies that work the best for their particular child:

- at different ages,
- at specific stages of development,
- whether behaviors are minor or severe,
- taking into account the child's individual personality.

The *discipline gradient* is a scale which rates the major discipline techniques according to their ability to teach internal controls, or self-discipline. Techniques listed near the beginning of the gradient prevent discipline problems from occurring in the first place, or use communication to solve problems. Prevention and communication techniques not only teach self-discipline; they also increase self-esteem and encourage warm family relationships.

However, sometimes prevention and communication techniques do not adequately resolve a problem. In these cases, techniques farther up the gradient are able to change behavior quickly. Punishment techniques are not taught in this book, but they are included and discussed to show their position as part of the whole range of discipline techniques.

The first two chapters give an overview of parenting concerns, self-esteem and child development. The third chapter explains the discipline gradient. The central portion of the book outlines specific discipline techniques. Each strategy is explained separately, including why the technique is valuable and how and when to use the technique for children of different ages. Within the descriptions of each technique are suggestions to individually shape that technique to specific problems you may be experiencing with your child.

Examples and exercises are included after each discussion to help parents adapt techniques for their own specific use. Following the discussion of techniques are chapters about anger and stress, and making changes. I recommend reading the book from start to finish, starting with the overview of parenting and child development, since both of those topics influence which discipline techniques work best for which people. However, the book is also designed to serve as a resource, and the discussion of each discipline technique can be read independently.

Chapter 1

Why Children Behave the Way They Do: Heredity

"Nature vs. nurture"

Children's behavior is influenced by both heredity and environment. Heredity refers to the genetic makeup of a child—specific personality traits—and also to the general stages that children go through as they grow to adulthood. Environment refers to the home and school environments that influence child development. In the past, psychologists argued over whether heredity (nature) or environment (nurture) played the greatest part in how a child turned out. Today most psychologists agree that both heredity and environment interact in the formation of a child's personality. Both are important: a child is not a blank slate to be inscribed by the parents, but neither is she merely a product of heredity. A child's inborn personality influences her behavior and her relationship with her parents. But in turn, parents have a strong influence on the development of their children.

Heredity—Inborn Personality Traits

When I was a school teacher—before I had children of my own—I silently blamed parents for many of the behavioral problems I saw in my classroom. Indeed, some of my students came from homes where parents were not physically or emotionally available. These children had a very difficult time adjusting to school. But there were also situations where the personality of the child contributed to behavioral problems. I did not realize until I was a parent how much children's personalities can differ because of inborn characteristics. My first- and second-born daughters are as different as summer and winter; one's strengths are the other's weaknesses, and vice versa. Of all the parents I have talked with who have more than one child, only a small percentage believe their children have similar personalities. In most cases, their experiences match my own; their children have widely differing traits.

What this means is:

1. what works well with one child might not work at all with another child,
2. what one child can handle easily might be overwhelming for another child,
3. what is "equal" for siblings might not be "fair" for children with differing needs,
4. motivation and self-esteem factors will be different for each child.

Individual Differences

Cheerful	← →	Moody
Calm	← →	Excitable
Outgoing	← →	Fearful
Orderly	← →	Messy

Inborn personality traits can be diagrammed as a series of scales that intersect and blend into each other. One child might be very excitable, cheerful and messy. The child's sibling might be excessively neat, moody and fearful. A third sibling's traits might fall right in the middle.

Each child's personality is an individual combination of various characteristics. Stanley Turecki, in *The Difficult Child*, recognizes nine temperamental traits of children identified in the New York Longitudinal Study, begun in 1956, in which Drs. Alexander Thomas, Stella Chess, and Herbert Birch followed 133 people from infancy to young adulthood. A description of these traits shows the range of factors that combine to influence a child's personality.

- *Activity level:* A child may be calm by nature or constantly in motion.
- *Distractibility:* Some children focus easily. Other children are quickly distracted by motion in the environment, or even by their own thoughts.
- *Persistence:* A stubborn child finds it hard to relinquish a desire, while a compliant child is more easily persuaded.
- *Adaptability:* Some children deal more easily with transition and change, while others have a difficult time.

- *Approach/withdrawal:* A child may enjoy new places, people, food or clothes; or be cautious or frightened by new situations.
- *Intensity:* Some children, whether happy or unhappy, are loud. Others show their emotions more quietly.
- *Regularity:* A child may be predictable in patterns of eating, sleeping and bowel habits, or a child may have inconsistent habits.
- *Sensory threshold:* Some children are easily bothered or over-stimulated by sensory input: noise, lights, colors, smells, pain, tastes, heat or cold, even the feel of clothes. Others handle sensory stimulation without distress.
- *Mood:* Some children seem optimists or pessimists by nature. Some have wide mood fluctuations.

A child's characteristics may be found at one extreme or anywhere in between. Most children fluctuate within the medium range. As children grow and mature, many traits begin to soften.

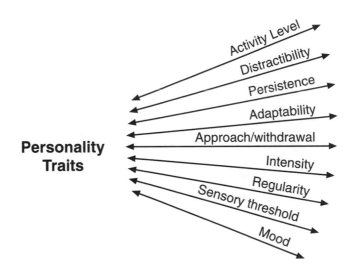

Personality differences can be viewed as varying levels of temperamental traits.

Hereditary factors are often responsible for specific personality traits. Although each child is unique, with unique needs and characteristics, it is useful to consider three personality types that may require an extra response on the part of the parent: the strong-willed child, the hypersensitive child and the shy child.

The strong-willed child is one who would always like to do something different than what the parent wants, or so it seems. She has strong ideas about what she wants or doesn't want; she demands reasons why, yet is rarely satisfied with those reasons. The strong-willed child is quick to become angry and carries grudges for a time, but often dismisses the incident completely when she is ready. She needs to save face. Even when she knows she is wrong or even when she *wants* to change her mind, she is unable to do so because then she would "lose." There are many similarities between strong-willed children and toddlers, who are working on independence issues and demanding power.

The Strong-Willed Child

needs personal power

does not back down
easily when confronted

quick to become angry,
can carry grudges, can
dismiss grudge quickly

needs to save face,
even when she is wrong

independence issues,
power struggles

rebellious

strong ideas, strong
opinions, knows what she
wants to do or not do

If you have a strong-willed child in your family:

1. Give appropriate personal power to your child. Whenever there are decisions that your child is capable of making, encourage her participation. Give her as much room for error as you can. For example, she can choose her own school clothes each day (or choose between outfits). Whenever possible, allow your child to learn through the use of natural consequences. If she insists she doesn't need her "show and tell" item (and you know she does), it may be painful, but she will live through it, and it will help her remember for the next time. See the sections on choices and natural consequences in chapter 5 for more ideas.

2. Teach responsibility for her actions. Your strong-willed child will try to wiggle out of consequences. The best thing you can do for her is to remain firm (no matter what) provided the consequence is fair. Giving in to strong-willed children because they simply wear us down actually teaches them to persist, even when they are in the wrong, because they know they can get their way. See chapter 8 for more information on logical consequences. Chapter 9 explains how to deal with children's "cons" using the "broken record"—helpful information when dealing with strong-willed children.

3. Give your strong-willed child space to change her mind. This tenet has brought the most peace to our household. When two of my children say "no" to a completely reasonable request, we have learned to save hours of painful conflict by allowing them time to change their minds. A parenting specialist once said we cannot force a child to do anything. All we can do is to decide how we ourselves will react to her behavior. When faced with a "No, I'm not going to!" by one of my strong-willed children, I frequently respond, "I'm sorry you feel that way. Perhaps you'll change your mind later." If the way has previously been prepared (that is, she knows the important reasons for doing the action but is just being stubborn), the child will usually respond if she is given time to think about it and the opportunity to change her mind without "losing." When she chooses to change her mind, she retains some personal power, and the parent is happy as well since the child is now doing the appropriate action. Knowing the consequence to a specific behavior, and knowing that mom or dad *will follow through* on that consequence, is integral to her decision.

4. Build a good relationship with your strong-willed child. This cannot be emphasized enough. A strong-willed child who does not have a good relationship with her parents has a great potential for running off on her own too young, too soon—making immature decisions that cause trouble. Unfortunately it is often hard to build a solid relationship with a strong-willed child, especially if the parent is a bit strong-willed herself (and remember, it tends to be hereditary). There is bound to be conflict. To encourage a positive relationship with your child:

- spend time alone with her in rewarding activities (see "Building Positive Relationships," chapter 4)
- talk to her; listen to her (see "Active listening" and "'I messages,'" chapter 6)

- encourage creative problem-solving (chapter 7)
- try to let go of perfectionism; allow her to choose her actions as much as possible, but be firm on the important rules
- enjoy her unique positive characteristics
- use humor to defuse discipline situations. One parent, when confronted with her child's refusal to do his chores, exclaimed, "Oh, I'm so glad you said that! I didn't want to make dinner anyway." Her son groaned at the reminder of shared responsibilities, but he did his chores.

Hints for the Strong-Willed Child

1. Give appropriate personal power to your child.
2. Teach responsibility for her actions.
3. Allow your strong-willed child space to change her mind.
4. Build a good relationship:
   - spend time alone with her in rewarding activities
   - talk to her; listen to her
   - encourage creative problem-solving
   - let go of perfectionism; allow her to choose her actions as much as possible, but be firm on the important rules
   - enjoy her unique positive characteristics
   - use humor to defuse discipline situations

The hypersensitive child does not have the normal behavioral controls most children have in response to stimuli. His sensory threshold is low; he is easily overstimulated and overreacts. He might be fearful and withdrawn, or frustrated and aggressive, or have a combination of these traits. The hypersensitive child has a high activity level: he is restless, squirms a lot and may be prone to accidents. He is an intense child: everything is important and he frequently responds with high-intensity reactions of screaming, crying or shrieking with delight. The hypersensitive child has problems with regularity; he has no inner sense of time and frequently wakes at night. These children tend to withdraw from new experiences and fear strangers. They do not adapt well. Not only do they dislike change, but they need a long time to adjust to new situations. And perhaps hardest of all to deal with, hypersensitive children frequently sport a negative mood. They tend to be fussy infants, whining toddlers and moody school-age children.

Turecki, in *The Difficult Child*, identifies the above qualities in newborns as high activity level, high intensity, irregularity, low sensory threshold, poor adaptability, initial withdrawal, and negative mood. These same traits can be found in hypersensitive children, modified slightly as they grow older.

The Hypersensitive Child

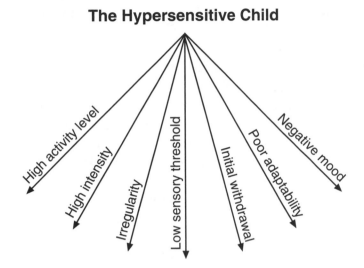

Hypersensitive children vary tremendously in their personality characteristics and in their relationships with their environment.

Some useful approaches to hypersensitivity include:

1. *Reduce the amount of sensory stimuli in your child's environment.* Hypersensitive children are often unable to edit the stimuli they encounter, nor do they have the control to respond to the ordinary stimuli most children handle every day. It is difficult for a hypersensitive child to tune out background noise; sensory input from all directions clamors for attention. The harder a baby fusses or cries, the greater the parent's tendency to rock a little faster, sing a little louder, hug him a little closer. Yet for a hypersensitive baby, too much stimulation only compounds the problems. He needs less stimulation, not more. You might try laying him in his bed and stroking his tummy lightly, avoiding eye contact and dimming the lights. Other hypersensitive babies

respond to voice, music or silence. Some like to lie with bare skin against a sheepskin. By experimenting, you can find out what your baby is most sensitive to and what calms him the fastest.

Use the same concept as the child grows: don't plan huge birthday parties under bright lights, try not to cram in last-minute shopping when the child is tired, help your child to calm himself before bedtime, and provide quiet places for homework.

2. Anticipate problem times and problem situations for your child. If your child has a difficult time handling scary movies and books, limit his exposure to them in your home. Share this knowledge with teachers and parents of his friends.

Expect that some times will be more stressful and your child will have a harder time. Be on hand for dentist appointments, pre-concert jitters, camping trips and other situations where your presence will help your child. Talk with your child to prepare him for new situations. See the discussion of anticipation in chapter 4.

3. Identify situations that set off your child. Choose one situation to problem-solve (see chapter 7). For example, if your child tends to fly out of control in sibling arguments, concentrate for a period of time on the building of social skills, without trying to solve everything else simultaneously.

4. Use behavior-management techniques, especially positive reinforcement. These work very well with hypersensitive children (see chapter 8).

5. Emphasize routine and consistency. Familiarity will help limit the chaos hypersensitive children experience in their sensory worlds.

Hints for the Hypersensitive Child

1. Reduce the amount of sensory stimuli in your child's environment.
2. Anticipate problem times and situations for your child; reduce or eliminate them if possible.
3. Identify situations that set off your child. Focus on changing one at a time.
4. Use behavior-management techniques, especially positive reinforcement.
5. Emphasize routine and consistency.

The shy child is oversensitive to people and social situations around her, frequently withdrawing as a response to fear and uncertainty. Different degrees of shyness affect many children. Shyness becomes a problem when a child is not able to establish relationships with other people, and when the shyness hinders her from developing in satisfying ways.

About 40 percent of teens and adults describe themselves as shy and unable to make satisfying contact with others. At age six, my son described shyness as "lots of people looking at you" and "feeling left out." Shy children feel exposed to the world and fear they don't measure up to people's expectations. Shy children, if left alone, will remain shy. They need help from others to discover that the world can be a friendly place, they will not shatter if they speak in a group, and others are shy too.

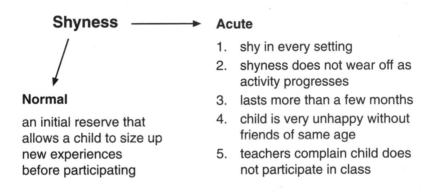

Shyness ⟶ **Acute**

1. shy in every setting
2. shyness does not wear off as activity progresses
3. lasts more than a few months
4. child is very unhappy without friends of same age
5. teachers complain child does not participate in class

Normal

an initial reserve that allows a child to size up new experiences before participating

Here are some things parents can do to help their shy children:

1. Teach social skills. Teach children how to make friends by smiling, introducing themselves by name, making eye contact, listening, and giving and accepting compliments. Make suggestions. "If looking at a person's eyes is too hard, look at his chin." Explain how others think and feel. "Children like it when you give them a turn." Avoid long periods of solitary television-watching. Provide play experiences with one or two other children; invite a friend to your house so your child is able to start out learning a new skill in a familiar environment.

2. Help a child deal with and move away from shyness in small steps. Prepare your child for new situations by explaining beforehand or by pairing her with a friend. Avoid putting your child in the spotlight;

don't push a solo in the school choir until the child is genuinely interested on her own. Encourage written communication with teachers and peers. Provide one-on-one opportunities for work, study and play.

3. Encourage supervised group experiences. A supportive group experience such as being part of a Girl Scout troop, a soccer team, or a computer club can do wonders for developing social skills in a shy child. As part of a small, continuous group, your child can get to know a small group of peers and another adult to model after. As contact increases, fear decreases. My shy older daughter has made tremendous social progress by participating in a Girl Scout troop over a period of many years. A few close troop friends support her in Girl Scout activities and also at school. Now in eighth grade, she is beginning to make friends in a wider circle, and is stretching her social skills to get to know her classmates better.

4. Encourage skill development. The more confident a shy child feels about her abilities, the less afraid she will feel. If your child works hard at playing a band instrument, or learning to ski or swim, she will feel more confident in school or social situations containing those activities. If tasks are difficult, break them into steps and work at mastering the first step. Experiences of success build confidence.

5. Teach positive self-talk. Negative self-talk (that quiet voice inside us that says "I'm dumb, I'm stupid, I can't") perpetuates shyness. The opposite is also true: positive self-talk defeats shyness. Suggest specific phrases your child might tell herself. "I have good ideas too" or "I can do it" or "I am worthwhile."

6. Role-play difficult situations. Act out aggressive peer situations at home and practice different responses. Empower the child by helping her to resolve difficult situations (rather than stepping in and resolving them for her). Use puppets with younger children. Shy children often freely put their own words into a puppet's mouth even when they are not able to express feelings on their own.

7. Provide a warm, accepting atmosphere. Let your child know that her family is always there to support her. Give help and suggestions sensitively and freely. Encourage mistakes (that's how we learn) rather than perfectionism, which inhibits learning and growth.

Pushing a shy child into outgoing behaviors is not useful and tends to cause harm: poor self-esteem, resentment or increased withdrawal.

How can a parent tell the difference between encouragement and pushing?

A pushy parent treats shyness as a negative trait to be eradicated, and shows his disapproval of shy behaviors in a way that discourages his child, causing poor self-esteem and strained relationships.

An encouraging parent takes his cue from his child, providing opportunities and strategies to help the shy child interact more comfortably within her world. An encouraging parent is always there to listen, to guide if the child asks, to support a shy child's decisions and to suggest alternate ways of achieving goals.

Emphasizing and enjoying a child's positive characteristics gives parents a fresher appreciation of the wonder of a child, and actually helps the child grow in the direction of that appreciation. Shy children often have a greater sensitivity to the world around them, which can be a positive by-product of shyness. This greater awareness might lead to greater creativity, artistic endeavor or scientific investigation.

Hints for the Shy Child

1. Teach social skills.
2. Help a child deal with shyness and move away from it in small steps.
3. Encourage supervised group experiences.
4. Encourage skill development.
5. Teach positive self-talk.
6. Role-play difficult situations.
7. Provide a warm, accepting atmosphere.

Whether or not a child fits into one of the above categories—strong-willed, hypersensitive or shy—is less important than our openness as parents to accept, encourage and support our children. Most children experience cycles of self-fulfilling behaviors. If the cycle is positive, the child grows, becoming more confident and self-assured. If the cycle is negative, the child can be locked into destructiveness. Destructive cycles almost never go away by themselves; the child must have the help of an adult to break the cycle.

Negative Self-Reinforcing Cycle

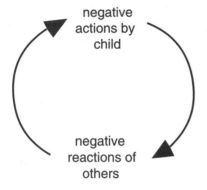

negative
actions by
child

negative
reactions of
others

A child who does poorly in school and makes social mistakes will receive negative reactions to his actions: failing grades, fewer opportunities for friendship, perhaps even ridicule. The negative reactions from others produce lowered self-esteem, which produces negative ideas: "I can't do it; I'll never have friends; I'm a poor student." The negative beliefs in turn cause more negative actions in a self-reinforcing cycle.

Positive Self-Reinforcing Cycle

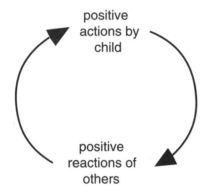

positive
actions by
child

positive
reactions of
others

A child who does well in school and interacts well with his peers will receive positive reactions to his actions: high grades, increasing opportunities for friendship, popularity. The positive reactions from others produce increased self-esteem, which produces positive ideas: "I can do it; I'm a good friend; I'm a good student." The positive beliefs in turn cause more positive actions in a self-reinforcing cycle. The positive nature of this cycle encourages a child to explore, risk and grow.

Not only can we as parents keep in mind our child's specific personality strengths, weaknesses and needs, but we can also advocate for our child in school, medical and other situations. If we have a hypersensitive child who has a difficult time in clinics and hospitals, it is our right and responsibility to stay beside her during most types of treatment. It is valuable to consult with professionals about our children's health and schooling, and we can gain objective information which is useful for our children. However, a genuinely concerned parent will have intuitive knowledge about her child that a professional may not have discovered yet. We can trust that knowledge and share it to help doctors, teachers and other professionals work most effectively with our children.

Heredity—Developmental Stages

The second part of nature—or hereditary reasons why children behave—is the developmental stages of growth that normal children pass through on their way to adulthood.

The diagram below combines Abraham Maslow's hierarcy of needs with Erik Erikson's developmental stages to present a picture of a child's emotional development at different ages.

Maslow's Hierarchy of Human Needs with Erikson's Developmental Tasks

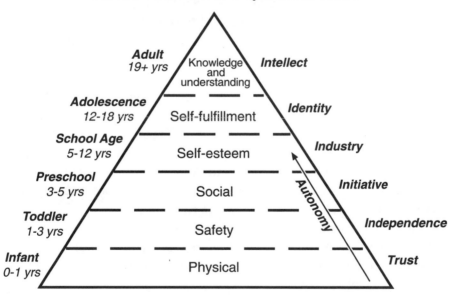

Maslow's hierarchy of needs is depicted inside the triangle. Erikson's developmental tasks are shown on the outside of the triangle.

By studying healthy people, Maslow theorized humans have certain basic needs that are hierarchical; that is, the first one must be met before the next one is worked on, and so forth. The first needs at the bottom of the pyramid are physical: air, food, water, warmth. After these are met, safety issues become most important. Safety includes not only physical safety, but also safety from too much chaos. Organization and routine can fit under this category. After safety needs are met, love and belonging needs become important, then self-esteem needs and self-fulfillment needs. (Exceptions to the hierarchy also exist; e.g., a mountain climber sacrifices personal safety for self-fulfillment needs.)

Erikson theorized that each stage of development carries with it a corresponding *task* the child is trying to accomplish. Babies are learning to trust that their needs will be met and that the world is a safe place. Toddlers are asserting independence, preschoolers are taking initiative, school-age children are industrious, and teens are forming identities.

Not every task is mastered at the right stage; not every basic need is met hierarchically. If a child does not fulfill a need or task at a specific stage, he will continue to work on it in the following stages. For example, if a child has not established trust in the first year of life, he will still progress into the second stage of creating independence, but the task will be a little harder and take a little longer, since he is working on two tasks simultaneously.

Even if he does master the task of each developmental stage on schedule, a child may slip back into an earlier stage—what we call regression—when under stress. Adults also regress. If we lose our job, we often slip into the love and belonging stage as we look for a shoulder to cry on, someone who cares and believes in us. If we face a larger loss—such as the death or divorce of a loved one—we might regress to the earlier physical needs stage. We may take to our beds for a day or a week to regroup, to recover. But most of us don't remain in the earlier stage. We gather ourselves together, fulfill our needs as we learn to deal with the stressful situation, and move back up into our appropriate age level.

Children similarly regress when under stress. For example, when a baby sister arrives from the hospital, a three-year-old boy may increase whining, want to drink milk from a bottle or forget his toilet training. Instead of trying to push the three-year-old back up the pyramid—by trying to get him to act his age—a sensitive parent will realize what her preschooler is searching for: time and comfort, physical touch from his parents and a trust that his world is still a good place.

By offering understanding ("It's hard to be a big brother when the baby cries so much and demands mom's attention"), hugs and involvement in the baby's care, the parent is responding to the current needs of the child and will help him adjust more quickly.

Knowing a child's developmental stage helps a parent gear expectations appropriately. One of the hardest tasks of parenting is to allow a child growth and independence. Or, stated another way, one of the hardest tasks of parenting is letting go. On the previous diagram, an arrow shows the direction of increasing autonomy. As the child grows in age and emotional development, the parent's task is to give the child the skills he needs to separate from his parents and home.

Infancy: The first major separation between mother and child occurs during childbirth. The physical union present during pregnancy—the mother's knowledge of her child's wakefulness, movement, shape—is over. The emotional bonds begun during pregnancy now have a focus for developing into relationships.

Infants are born with the ability to use all five senses. Studies have shown that even before birth, babies in the mother's uterus are able to hear and respond to touch. Newborns have demonstrated strong senses of smell and taste. A newborn's sight is limited to tunnel vision, and is clearest at a distance of about ten to twelve inches—just the characteristics needed to focus in on a parent's face when cradled in her arms. Babies in the first month of life are still learning to regulate their body cycles and systems—such as eating, elimination and sleep cycles.

Infant Developmental Issues

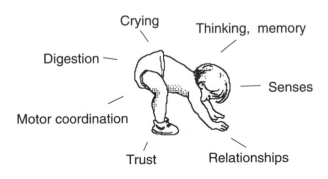

Crying

Thinking, memory

Digestion

Senses

Motor coordination

Trust

Relationships

As the baby grows older, his total dependency is tempered by milestones—such as interest in objects besides his mother's face, eating solid foods, crawling, walking and talking—that slowly begin his long climb toward self-sufficiency.

The physiological dependence of the baby's first year promotes a close relationship between parent and child. If the parent responds to the baby's needs, the baby begins to trust that his needs will be met. This is generalized to an understanding that the world is a good place, planting the seeds of self-esteem (not in thoughts, but in feelings): "I must be a good person because mom and dad come when I need them." Several decades ago it was thought that crying developed a baby's lungs, and that picking up a baby too much would spoil her. However, most physicians and child psychologists today recognize that a baby's cry is an effort to communicate a need, and they encourage new parents to pick up their babies when they cry. Infancy is a time to respond to your baby's needs, providing the security that leads to trust. Chapter 4 includes anticipating techniques that help to prevent discipline problems from arising. Substitution (chapter 5) is also a valuable technique to use with babies.

Toddlers: The first major cognitive/emotional separation occurs in the developing independence of the toddler. For the first time, the toddler distinguishes his own self as separate from his parents. As a baby, parents and caregivers seemed like extensions of his own needs, people to bring him food, warmth and cuddling. But a toddler can move away from his parents and caregivers. He can think and express thoughts that are his own. He can cause an action to happen. All the resulting contrariness can be a headache for mother and father, but it is also a sign of the healthy growth of independence. The toddler's two favorite words are "no!" and "mine!" The word "no" shows assertion and disagreement, signs of individuality. The word "mine" shows ownership, which also indicates the new separation between child and parents.

Because toddlers are working on establishing independence, a rule of thumb for toddlers would be *a few, firm limits.* A *few* limits, because your toddler is looking for excuses to assert himself. Parents who leave breakable knickknacks on low coffee tables are headed for arguments. Constant fighting strains the parent-child relationship. It is better to choose a few important rules—usually concerning safety and some socialization issues—and stick to these rules *firmly*. When the toddler sees that his parents will not give in, he learns to accept those limits.

Toddler Developmental Issues

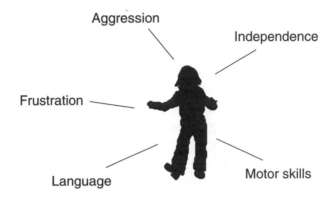

Aggression

Independence

Frustration

Language

Motor skills

Another way to help the toddler (and the parent) through this stage is to offer appropriate power to the child (see "Choices" and "Natural Consequences," chapter 5). Distracting choices are my favorite discipline technique for toddlers, since they offer acceptable personal power and distract the toddler from the main issue (which does not offer a choice), such as going to bed or leaving the playground.

I encourage parents of toddlers to let go of parental needs that are low on the priority list. Disciplining for too many situations weakens the parent-child relationship and causes frustration for both sides. It can also inhibit the toddler's natural drive to explore his world. "Baby-proofing" removes potential problems from the child's environment. Chapters 4 and 5 outline prevention techniques such as anticipating, which work well for avoiding problems with toddlers.

The "terrible twos" are so named for parents who must deal with contrary children, but it is an apt name for the toddler's troubles, too. Besides the task of separating from his parents, the toddler is learning and practicing many complex skills. He is perfecting his large and small motor skills—learning to run and climb without stumbling, putting on clothes and wrestling with zippers. His growing awareness of self makes him feel his needs acutely, but his stumbling progress in language skills is inadequate to express them. The natural result is increased aggression. When the pile of blocks falls, several are thrown in anguish. When the other child refuses to give up a toy, the toddler—lacking verbal skills—hits him and takes the toy. Aggression normally reaches its height in toddlerhood and then slowly declines with the growth of language.

Parents can help toddlers by limiting the amount of frustration they must handle. If the sky is about to fall and the tantrum about to erupt, a sensitive helping hand from mother or dad can save the day. The safety needs in Maslow's pyramid also refer to organization, orderliness and protection from too much frustration.

Preschoolers: The preschool-age child is broadening her world. Belonging to family and other groups such as extended family or preschool is one way of feeling assured that she is loved and cared for. The first peer friendships and cooperative play emerge. Having established her individuality, the preschooler initiates action to make an effect on her world. When preschoolers play together, you will hear suggestions: "Let's play school!" "Let's play house!" "Okay, I want to use the dress-up clothes." "You be the neighbor and I'll come to visit."

Preschool Developmental Issues

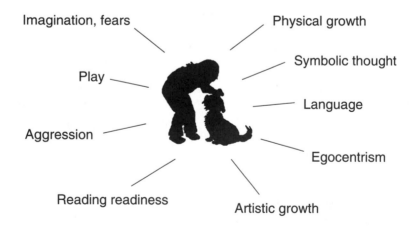

Imagination, fears — Physical growth — Symbolic thought — Play — Language — Aggression — Egocentrism — Reading readiness — Artistic growth

Parents can encourage their preschooler's initiative by offering manageable choices and allowing as many child-initiated options as possible. If your preschooler suggests that the family eat at a favorite restaurant, it will encourage her initiative if you occasionally act on her suggestion. Self-esteem is enhanced because her choice was recognized and welcomed. The separation between parent and child is slowly widening as the child becomes more competent, more able to appreciate herself, and better able to make choices.

Preschoolers are entering a whole new world of discovery as a major cognitive development occurs: symbolic thinking, which develops as language progresses. Words are symbols for people, places, things and actions; soon anything can be a symbol for something else. Whereas the toddler may play with one toy at a time, preschoolers often mix up the toy boxes: puzzle pieces become food on the play dishes at the stuffed animals' tea party. Imagination soars, and sometimes sails out of bounds. It is very common for preschoolers to go through a fearful stage and to have nightmares, since the dividing line between imagination and reality is not very clear at this stage. Technology—with color television and big-screen dramatic movies— helps blur the distinction between fantasy and reality. Is the dragon on the movie screen real or not? How about the dragon in her dream?

One year I had two preschoolers in my house. Jamie was nearly five years old, moving toward reality and away from fears; Steven was three and just beginning to fear the cartoon dragons on television. Once, when Steven cowered from a television character, Jamie explained with confidence in her growing awareness of what was real: "It's okay, Steven, they can't get out of the box!"

Parents of preschoolers can help nightmare problems by remaining calm and reassuring, providing nightlights and flashlights, and perhaps allowing the child a sleeping bag in the parents' room for emergency nightmares. Empowering a child works better than rescuing him. Reading picture books together about nightmares will often suggest strategies, such as making friends with the beast in the dream. As children grow into the school-age stage, nightmare problems tend to diminish.

Because of the unclear line between imagination and reality, imaginary friends often appear during the preschool years. It is best not to encourage the imaginary playmate with elaborate scenes or conversations. On the other hand, denying the existence of the imaginary friend tends to be ineffective or occasionally traumatic. It is probably best to accept the child's explanations matter-of-factly without further encouragement (e.g., good-humoredly moving to another chair if you've just sat on "Charlie," but not initiating questions on how

Charlie is doing this morning). Children generally know when to move on developmentally and leave their imaginary friends behind.

Preschoolers are still very egocentric, as are infants and toddlers. The whole world seems to center around themselves. But as preschoolers continue their cognitive growth, they begin the transition to understanding another point of view. This makes the preschool age a great time to teach creative problem-solving, described in chapter 7. Preschoolers also respond very well to logical consequences, explained in chapter 8.

School-age children: The seedling self-esteem that has budded in the first few stages of growth springs upward rapidly—or is hurtfully stunted—during the school-age years. School-age children, busy with the task of industry, are testing their abilities at many new things. The school environment encourages or discourages their academic achievement, creativity, motor skills, cooperation and special talents. Children of this age need opportunities to try many different activities. By experimenting, they find out what they are good at. The poor academic student may nourish his self-esteem on a sports team where he can shine. The uncoordinated child may excel at an individual artistic skill. The child who appears to excel at nothing might have a happy social life and be a great mediator. Parents can foster a child's self-esteem by encouraging all stages of an activity—not just by praising the accomplishment at the end. See chapter 2 for more discussion of self-esteem.

School-Age Developmental Issues

Sense of competence

Separation from family

Peer acceptance

Skill mastering: intellectual, physical, social

Growth away from egocentricity

More autonomy is achieved as children increase their skills and grow closer to the time when they will be responsible for their own choices. Signals of increasing independence include collection hobbies (possession implies ownership and individuality), secrets not shared with parents, "keep out" signs on doors to their rooms, a greater interest in peer activities (versus family activities), a secret girlfriend or boyfriend, and a healthy modeling relationship with other adults of the same sex, such as a teacher or parent of a friend.

The discipline technique of positive reinforcement (discussed in chapter 8) works very well for this age because school-age children enjoy systems, counting and organization. All four communication techniques discussed in chapters 6 and 7 are also excellent techniques for school-age children.

Teens: Suddenly a third major time of separation occurs. Teens must learn to separate from their parents, to form their own identities, and to become responsible for the major decisions of adulthood. Meanwhile, they are dealing with the strong, varying emotions that accompany active hormones and changing bodies. Many parents of teens become bewildered at the dramatic changes in their children. Teens don't seem to listen anymore. They spend all their time before the mirror in the bathroom, checking and changing their appearance, yet are unable to keep a semblance of neatness in their bedrooms. They are lost within themselves, contemplating their problems, but cannot appreciate the needs of others. They seem unable to form goals, and they make decisions on an emotional basis.

Teens practice decision-making and become comfortable with a cognitively broader view of life by arguing and challenging others (especially parents and teachers). When teens develop crushes on a girlfriend or boyfriend, they often take the seemingly finite love and loyalty that previously went to the family and bestow it on their friend. Their egocentrism, or self-centeredness, which disappeared somewhat during the school-age years, returns. Extreme self-consciousness characterizes teens, closely connected to changing bodies, changing voices, changing ideas. Teens have strong opinions, yet have a hard time following through on their own ideas. Many teens develop a personal religion—a private relationship with a Higher Power and an outlet for their deepest secrets.

For an in-depth discussion of teen traits and issues, read David Elkind's book *All Grown Up and No Place to Go*. The teen characteristics on the diagram below are similar to Elkind's organization of teen traits.

Teen Development Issues

Teens need time alone to figure out who they are. Adults tend to define themselves by occupation, gender and status, but teens discover who they are by figuring out their innermost characteristics and skills. Like toddlers, who are also going through a major separation stage, teens need firm limits on the important issues, but lots of freedom to make choices and decisions on other occasions. Having too many limits for teens causes the same dramatic effects as having too many limits for toddlers: rebellion, confrontations, strained relationships, or, less often, dependence. An excellent discipline technique for teens is contracts (see chapter 9). Contracts have a strong ability to shape teens' behavior without causing resentment or rebellion.

The real challenge of parenting teens is to let go, to allow your child to search for and accept the adult she will become. This task is much easier if you have spent time fostering your child's self-esteem and teaching decision-making skills at an earlier age. Positive self-esteem and a strong ability to make individual decisions (without following a crowd) are qualities that will help your children through the stormy teen years.

The developmental staircase

Just as separation occurs more acutely at certain stages, so do discipline problems. Throughout our lives, we all experience mastery of specific developmental skills (e.g., walking, toilet training, skipping, learning how to study, being hired for a job), which are usually preceded by the stress of learning them. Because children grow rapidly, they pass through many stages of mastering skills within a short period of time.

A baby must first learn to sit and crawl before she can walk. The periods immediately before these milestones often contain more fussiness, more crying, poorer eating habits, less ability to sleep through the night. After a milestone is reached, a plateau period of calm provides a welcome break from the stress of growing. For a time things go smoothly. Then the stress begins again as the baby prepares for the next growth spurt. The periods of stress/growth and calm can be diagrammed in a staircase:

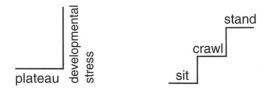

As adults, we still traverse periods of stress and plateaus, but our steps and our stressful periods tend to be longer. We might plateau at a comfortable job for years before feeling the need to change careers. Then we must deal with the stresses of searching for new avenues of interest, applying for new jobs or deciding to go back to school (the upward period of stress and learning). Eventually, after the decisions are made and the new job is found, we slide into an easier time, another plateau.

If parents recognize the stressful periods of children's growth, they can adjust their discipline strategies accordingly. It helps to know that after a stormy stage, a pleasant plateau is probably on the way. There are ups and downs to every stage, but no one can deny that some stages seem to have less equilibrium than others.

Although all normal children pass through the same stages, children go through them at their own rates of growth. How fast a child reaches a developmental stage is not related to his intelligence; he is just following the internal timetable he was born with. Generally speaking, girls tend to be developmentally ahead of boys by up to one year. (You might want to consider this when placing your child in kindergarten: the youngest boy can be up to two years behind the oldest girl in developmental issues.)

Below is a simplified sketch of ages and stages. If your three-year-old is going through a stressful time (instead of the plateau indicated for three-year-olds on the staircase chart), consider that she may be developmentally still in the toddler uphill climb. Or she may be already scrambling into the stressful fours. Once you figure out where your child is on the staircase, you can plot periods of stress and plateau.

The Developmental Staircase

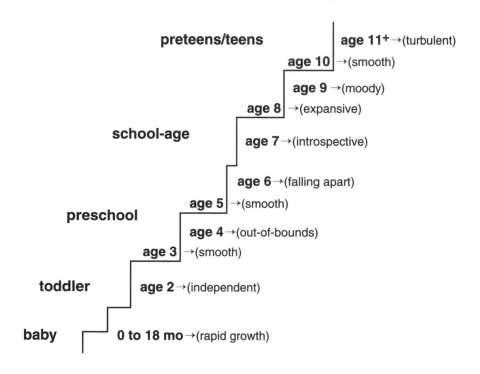

Individual differences will soften or strengthen an emotional stage. Jamie, my outgoing daughter, was not as introspective at age 7 as her shy sister. However, at age 8 Jamie pushed to the limits the meaning of the word "expansive."

Sometimes it is helpful just understanding that a discipline problem reflects a stage the child is going through. Perhaps no action needs to be taken, or at the least, we can worry less; he will probably grow out of it. Understanding the developmental causes of a child's stress can help the parent choose a discipline plan best for the child.

Chapter 2

Why Children Behave the Way They Do: Parenting Skills and Self-Esteem

In chapter 1, we discussed the "nature" part of why children behave the way they do, and how heredity affects children's inborn personality traits and stages of development. In this chapter, we will consider the "nurture" part of children's behavior—how parents influence their children's behavior and self-esteem.

Environment and Parenting Skills—Modeling, Nurturing and Discipline

Parents generally can't do much to change their children's personality or development. But parents can help their children deal with inborn traits by providing a supportive environment.

Three skills are required in parenting: modeling, nurturing and discipline. The three skills are interrelated and overlapping (for example, the way we nurture also models nurturing). Somewhere in the intersection between the three skills lies parental influence on the child's self-esteem.

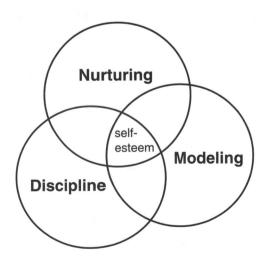

Modeling

Children learn by watching or imitating. Have you ever seen your child act like you or your partner? Have you ever heard your words coming out of your child's lips? One mother says that's how she quit swearing.

"I was so angry (during a phone conversation), I couldn't help myself. I slammed the phone down and started muttering my favorite swear phrase. My husband hates it when I use that phrase in front of my two-year-old daughter, who was looking out the window, so I bit it off halfway. For a moment everything was silent. Then a very small voice finished the phrase."

Everything we do is modeled to our children. One of the strongest influences is the way spouses or partners interact. Some research studies indicate that the strength of the mother-father (or partner) bond is the most influential factor in whether or not a child "turns out all right." Our relationships with our partner, our children and non-family members have an important influence on what our children's relationships will be like in the future.

Very young children—babies and toddlers—imitate everything they see their parents do, from eating habits to anger responses. Imitation is one of the first techniques young children use to interpret their world. The cognitive understanding that the parents' way is not the only way does not appear until the school-age stage, and sometimes not even until the teen years.

Think back to your own childhood. What is something that you learned from your parents or caregivers, either positive or negative, that they never told you? One mother relates that she learned females played subservient roles, even though their family never talked about it. Growing up on a farm, she worked alongside her brothers at hard physical labor but was never allowed to run the machinery. It was inferred the men were not only smarter, but also needed to protect the women against possible physical harm. Coming in late at night after working hard all day, the men sat down to eat and the women served them. Sundays were the men's day of rest, but the women caught up on sewing and laundry. As an adult, this woman realized she had a choice of what she could teach her children about male and female roles. She consciously decided to model a more equal version of gender roles.

Our early experiences of being parented when we were children often influence us as parents in ways that we may not be aware of. We may do something simply because it's the way we've always done it (or the way our parents handled it), and not necessarily because we want to keep it as part of our parenting repertoire.

The old story comes to mind of the wife who always cut off the ends of the pot roast before baking it. When her husband asked why, she said her mother had always done it. The couple asked the woman's mother why she had always cut off the ends of the pot roast, and the woman's mother replied that *her* mother had always done it. When the grandmother was consulted, she explained that her pan was too small, and the pot roast would never fit unless she cut off both ends first. The moral—which is also valid for parenting skills—is that evaluating old ways of doing things in the light of current needs will help us decide which techniques we want to keep and which we want to throw out.

The exercise that follows is designed to help a parent remember what modeling taught him as a child, and to see how he would like to use modeling in his current family.

Modeling Exercise

Modeling is parental action that a child learns by watching or imitating. It can be negative or positive.

1. What is one thing you learned from your parents that they didn't tell you in words?

2. How did you learn that? (What was the nonverbal behavior?)

3. What do you want your child(ren) to learn about that topic?

4. What actions will you do to model and teach it?

Modeling begins very early. It involves speech patterns and gestures as well as behavior.

5. List several things your child already does that imitate you or other persons in your family.

6. List two habits or traits you or your spouse have that you hope your child will pick up.

7. List two habits or traits you or your spouse have that you hope your child will not pick up.

Modeling

Nurturing

Nurturing often comes naturally to parents; offering love and receiving it in return is one of the rewards of parenting. The word "nurture" comes from the root "to nourish." When a parent nourishes a child's heart, soul, mind and body, the child feels loved; he perceives that he is respected, enjoyed, appreciated. The child's self-esteem grows positively.

But nurturing is not always instinctive, especially if the child is difficult to deal with in some way. Perhaps she is strong-willed or hypersensitive, or her personality just doesn't mix well with the personality of the parent.

With older children's emerging sexuality, parents are often afraid to offer the hugs and kisses they frequently gave their toddlers. Some psychologists wonder if the growing statistics regarding teen premarital sex might be related to the lack of appropriate touch teens receive.

All people need touch. Studies done in orphanages in the 1950s tragically pointed out that babies must have touch in order to survive. Babies who were touched and held thrived; those who were not (although their basic needs were met), lost the will to live.

Teens also need to be touched and held. Parents can offer appropriate touch to their teens through backrubs, hugs, foot or scalp massages, touching hands, or an arm around the shoulders.

There are also many nonphysical ways to nurture a child. Almost all nurturing includes giving time and attention. Perhaps the greatest desire of a child is attention from his parent. Whenever the parent is available to devote his full attention to the child, a clear message arises: you are important to me. Spending time alone with a child is one of the best ways to nurture him.

Reading to your child not only nurtures his self-esteem, but also provides one of the strongest factors in whether or not a child will learn to read well himself. Don't stop reading to your children once they can read on their own; let them read to you sometimes, and continue reading out loud to them. The pleasure of hearing a story never fades; plus the child is able to hear and interpret difficult words and ideas in context.

The exercise that follows is designed to help a parent remember how she was nurtured as a child, and to clarify what types of nurturing she would like to use with her own children.

Nurturing Exercise

1. How did my parents show they loved me...
   as a young child?

   as a school-age child?

   as a teenager?

2. When did my parents show they loved me (at what times during the day, the week, the year, my life)?

Nurturing

3. What did touching mean in our family? Was it warm and nurturing? Did it happen often? Was it hurtful?

4. How do I want my children to feel about touching?

5. What did my parents say to me that helped build my self-esteem?

6. What did my parents say to others about me that helped build my self-esteem?

7. What are my favorite ways of nurturing my children?

8. What are some types of nurturing I would like to add in my family?

Discipline

Discipline helps a child move from external controls to internal controls. When children are babies and toddlers, a large amount of parental (external) control is required to keep them safe and to provide the best opportunities for their growth. As teens, however, children are turning outward to their peers and inward to their own emerging sense of identity. Parents are heeded less by teens reaching for independence. Ideally, somewhere between infants and teens occurs the gradual growth of self-discipline. Effective external discipline builds internal controls.

Discipline is not the same as punishment. Punishment—retribution or penalty—is a form of discipline, but it is often hurtful and is not very effective at establishing internal controls in children. In addition, it tends to erode self-esteem for both parents and children, and it weakens parent-child relationships. For these reasons it is included at the far end of the discipline gradient. Chapter 10 discusses punishment, how it differs from discipline and why it is less effective than other techniques.

Webster defines discipline as "an activity, exercise or a regimen that develops or improves a skill." Effective discipline develops the skills of self-control, problem-solving and decision-making. In this context, communication and prevention techniques also fit under discipline.

What were the discipline and punishment techniques you experienced as a child? Do you use the same techniques with your own children? How we were disciplined as children often greatly influences the way we discipline our own children. The following exercise allows a closer look at your discipline strategies and gives you the chance to determine what you would like to continue and what you might like to change.

Discipline Exercise

1. How was I disciplined when I was a child?

2. What negative consequences occurred when I disobeyed? How did they make me feel?

3. What positive discipline situations occurred? How did they make me feel?

4. Was I allowed to tell my parents how I felt?

5. How do I feel about the way discipline was handled?

Discipline

6. Do I discipline my children the way I was disciplined? In what ways?

7. What do I want to teach when I discipline my children?

8. What do I like about the way I discipline my children?

9. What would I like to change about the way I discipline my children?

Self-Esteem: Through the Eyes of the Child

We hear so much about self-esteem from teachers and magazines and talk shows. Is it really so important?

When we analyze the decisions a person makes, first as a child, then as a teenager and an adult, it becomes clear that self-esteem influences virtually all decisions in life. Depending on how they feel about themselves, children choose whether or not to answer questions in class, to turn in homework, to keep a promise, to form a friendship or to cheat on a test. Studies show that children and teens with a strong sense of positive self-esteem are least influenced by peer pressure regarding alcohol, drugs or premarital sex. In addition, how teens feel about themselves influences major decisions that will mold their futures—the choices of career, job, trade school or university, mates, home and children.

Children who feel worthy of love and respect seek relationships which offer love and respect. Confident children choose activities that boost their confidence. But children who see themselves as lacking worthiness or ability tend to choose relationships and activities that increase their negative opinions of themselves. Each cycle is self-reinforcing (see the self-reinforcing diagrams in chapter 1).

Our personal image of ourselves is greatly influenced by the people around us—not necessarily by what those people actually think about us, but by how we perceive they think about us.

In the diagram of the three parenting skills on page 27, self-esteem is found in the intersection of modeling, nurturing and discipline. When all three skills interact in the positive interests of the child, self-esteem increases not only for the child, but also for the parents, who become more confident in their parenting.

Even though nurturing most directly impacts children's self-esteem, the other two skills have a profound effect: the child sees her image in the mirror of her parents' actions. A parent may truly love her child, yet be unable to show her love due to her own insecurities. If her child perceives a lack of love (even though he really is loved), that perception hinders the development of positive self-esteem.

Morgan's mother, for example, thought her daughter was very pretty. However, Mrs. Green thought it would influence her daughter's sex-role development if she offered too much praise of Morgan's femininity. As a result, Mrs. Green was very careful *not* to compliment her daughter's looks, especially when Morgan was wearing dresses, curls or makeup. Because of the lack of communication in this area, Morgan inferred that something was wrong with her looks, and that she was not pretty or desirable.

Although each child is influenced by many mirrors of perceived acceptance, the first, most important mirror is provided by the child's parents or early caregivers. To build positive self-esteem, parents and caregivers must be able to express their caring so the child understands he is loved. This is significant: love alone is not enough; expressing that love is equally necessary.

Criticism tends to make a person feel insecure or defensive. If someone in authority frequently tells us we are doing poorly—or even worse, that we are inherently stupid or inept—we begin to seriously doubt our abilities. Our self-confidence erodes; we become fearful of tackling new responsibilities or of reaching out to others.

On the other hand, if a tactful boss praises a worker periodically, specifically mentioning accomplishments not long after they are completed, the worker feels pride and redoubles his efforts to do well.

Children have similar reactions when scolded or praised. Yet we frequently tell our children what they are doing wrong and forget to tell them what they are doing right. In addition, criticism pointed toward the child is more hurtful than criticism directed toward the child's action. If we frequently remark within Jon's hearing that he is stupid and irresponsible, we will eventually convince him that he is those things. Children—especially young children—tend to see adults as all-powerful. What parents say must be true.

Jon stands a good chance of living up to his parents' expectations. "I can't get good grades—I'm stupid," say the internal voices. "I always seem to break the rules—I'm irresponsible." Self-esteem drops; Jon makes more mistakes; external criticism and his own internal voices tell him even more clearly how stupid he is...the cycle tightens.

Tactful criticism can be a learning experience, especially if combined with other positive approaches. But reducing criticism and increasing encouragement will build self-esteem instead of destroying it.

Parents and caregivers are the first mirrors to a child's self-esteem, but other influences play a part. Television and other media glamorize the young, strong, slim and beautiful. Teachers, grandparents and other influential adults may influence a child's perception of herself. Peer opinions become more and more important as a child grows older and begins the natural process of separating from the family. Parents are not able to control all the elements that affect their child, especially as she grows older. But parents will always have the ability to impact how their child feels about herself.

Four-year-old Mandy was coloring happily by herself, so her mother went into the next room to make a long-distance phone call. Halfway through, Mandy raced into the room, crying, "Mom, Mom, look what I made!" Her mother signaled her to leave the room, but Mandy insisted that her mother look at her picture.

Mandy's mother hung up the phone. Fuming, she faced her daughter and shouted, "How many times have I told you not to interrupt me during a phone call!"

The energy dispersed from Mandy, who stood silently, still holding out her picture. Her shoulders drooped, her arms fell to her sides, the picture forgotten. She looked at her shoes. "Sorry, Mom," she said in a small voice.

How many times have I told you not to interrupt me?

How many times have we parents reacted from an adult viewpoint, allowing our own pressures to suppress a child's enthusiasm for life?

Often we are so filled with our own needs and stresses that we don't notice our child's viewpoint. Occasionally we are so angry we don't care (see chapter 11 for more about anger and stress). Many times we do notice, but it is too late. We kick ourselves mentally and tell ourselves we will do it differently next time. But next time we are still unprepared. In today's often hectic world, it is hard to pull out the right responses to our children's actions.

Dorothy Corkille Briggs, author of *Your Child's Self-Esteem*, explains that children find their self-esteem in the mirrors of the people around them. Briggs divides self-esteem into two parts: a feeling of being worthwhile, lovable for oneself; and a feeling of competence and confidence.

I think of these two aspects as the "I am" and the "I can" aspects. "I am lovable" and "I can do something well." Both parts need to be nourished for positive self-esteem.

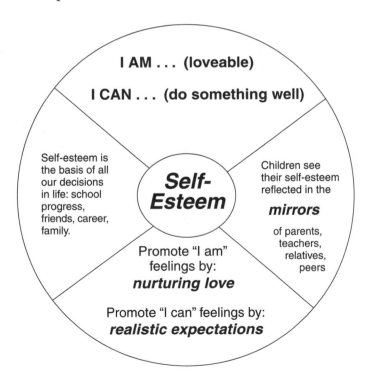

The "I am" part of self-esteem needs positive nurturing to blossom effectively. All the ideas covered earlier under the discussion of nurturing will nourish a child's feelings of being worthwhile just for being himself.

The "I can" part of self-esteem requires realistic expectations of the child, as well as a confident attitude that the child will succeed. Unrealistic expectations tend to fall into three types: too low, too high, or dependent on the parent's needs.

Expectations that are too low. If the adult expects little or nothing of the child, the child tends to meet those expectations, achieving little or nothing. In addition, the child receives the message "I don't believe you can do it." A natural response is "Why try if I'm not able to do it?"

Expectations that are too high. If expectations on the part of parent or teacher are consistently too high, the child tends to set up unrealistically high expectations for himself. When he has a hard time meeting those high goals on a regular basis, the child concludes that he is not good enough.

Expectations dependent on the parent's needs. Sometimes parents set up unrealistic expectations for their children that are connected to the parents' own goals. A mother may push her daughter into ballet lessons or art classes because the mother feels unfulfilled about her own childhood opportunities. A father may want his son to follow in his footsteps regarding career goals. If these children are pushed into activities and careers they do not really want, they will find themselves competing with highly motivated peers. Unable to match the energy of the children around them, unmotivated children compare themselves to their peers and come up short.

To be *realistic,* an expectation must meet three conditions:
1. it must take into consideration knowledge of general child development,
2. it must consider specific information about the child, usually discovered by individual observation, and
3. it must take into consideration any stresses which are acting on the child.

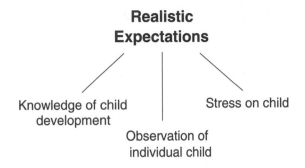

Realistic Expectations

Knowledge of child development

Observation of individual child

Stress on child

Knowledge of general child development helps a parent understand how a child's actions are influenced by his age and developmental level. A tantrum thrown by a two-year-old is different from a tantrum thrown by an eight-year-old. Knowing that age 2 is often characterized by frustration and strong bids for independence will help a parent decide what to expect of a child of this age. A hungry, tired two-year-old child who throws a tantrum is probably acting like a typical two-year-old. However, an eight-year-old who deliberately throws a tantrum to get her way is not acting within the normal behaviors of her age level.

If a parent is not knowledgeable about developmental issues, any tantrum may be seen as a huge problem. The parent may expect too much of a two-year-old—being in a good mood at a luncheon when she has had to skip her nap, for example. Or the parent may not realize that the eight-year-old's tantrum might indicate a deeper problem.

Knowledge of specific information about a child also helps the parent build appropriate expectations. A child's individual temperament greatly influences how she will react in a given situation. Will eight-year-old Rebecca recite a poem for her parents' dinner party? If Rebecca is outgoing and enjoys the limelight, she is probably willing and charming. If Rebecca is shy or fearful, she may act sullen and withdrawn.

Is it realistic to expect a shy, fearful child to be chosen for the lead role in the school play? Even though eight-year-olds generally tend to be outgoing and expressive, a very shy eight-year-old will still have a hard time dealing with situations demanding group expression. Sensitive parents will take this into consideration when they consider their expectations for their child's role in the school play. (General child development and individual temperament are discussed more fully in chapter 1.)

Besides general and specific information about a child's developmental level and temperament, parents must consider one more influence: *what is the level of stress the child is operating under?* Just as stress influences the health and performance of adults, so it weakens a child's ability to think and act effectively. We might not think of stress as a large factor in children's lives. Stress is what adults deal with: finances, relationships, career decisions. But children also operate under a daily burden of stress, which is sometimes overlooked by adults.

What are a child's daily stressors? Homework, being called on in class, being teased by peers, practicing for sports and other extracurricular activities, daycare, transitions between school and home, sibling rivalry, going to the dentist, and being hurried from one thing to another, to name a few. In addition, there are larger transitional stresses that children face: returning to school after vacations, moving to a new school or home, repeating a grade, a new sibling joining the family, the absence of a parent, separation and divorce, adjusting to a stepparent and stepsiblings. (Chapter 11 discusses how adults can help children deal with stress.)

Realistic expectations take into account the stress on a child. A normally outgoing Rebecca, in the midst of an outgoing developmental phase, may not be ready to compete for the leading role in the school play if she has just moved to a new community and started going to a new school.

Parents who take into consideration their child's general developmental stage, her specific personality traits, and her level of stress will be able to form expectations that are realistic. Realistic expectations help children build the "I can" part of positive self-esteem.

Children take their cue from adults: what parents and teachers expect of them, they are also likely to expect of themselves. If children are able to form realistic expectations, their chances of meeting their goals are very good. Success leads to positive feelings about oneself, which leads to more successes.

Chapter 3

The Discipline Gradient

We will not always be around to control our children or to help them to control themselves. But we can give our children the motivation and self-control that results from effective discipline. Discipline comes from the word *disciple*, meaning "to learn." Effective discipline teaches decision-making and problem-solving skills, and guides children from external (parental) controls to internal controls, or self-discipline.

Troubled parents are often stuck in repetitive patterns of discipline that are no longer working. To shake free of these patterns, new techniques can be learned to teach children internal controls and to build rapport between parent and child. When a child develops internal controls, everybody wins. The child takes steps toward independence and adulthood. The parent relaxes as the problem behavior is resolved. Parents and children get along better. The self-esteem of the child is enhanced because the child takes responsibility for behavior and gains a sense of personal power. The self-esteem of the parent is enhanced as the parent's new knowledge and skills lead to improved child behavior and better rapport.

To be effective, discipline should:

1. help a child move from external (parental) controls to internal controls (self-discipline),
2. allow the child to grow and develop his potential characteristics and skills, and
3. enhance the parent-child relationship.

If a parent has a limited repertoire of discipline techniques, it is easy to fall back on only one or a few ways of handling behavior problems. But relying on only one child management technique can be dangerous at worst and ineffective at best. Discipline situations are different, children are different, and no one technique solves every problem satisfactorily. In addition, the technique chosen might build resentment and rebellion (as many punishment techniques do). In this case, discipline becomes a battle, a continuous confrontation, and the parent-child relationship begins to erode.

A tool called *the discipline gradient* can be used to organize a wide range of discipline techniques according to how well they encourage internal controls, and according to how severe the problem is. A *gradient* is a slope showing a gradual change by steps or stages from one condition to another. The discipline gradient organizes discipline techniques according to four areas: prevention, communication, behavior management and punishment.

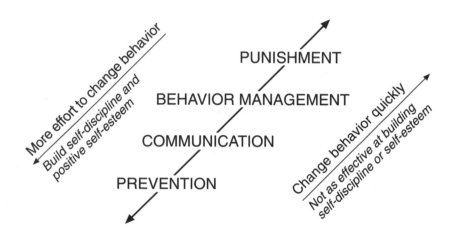

For each area, I have selected four or five specific discipline techniques which are strong and have lasted over time. Techniques on the lower end of the gradient (prevention and communication) are best at building self-discipline and positive self-esteem. Techniques on the upper end of the gradient (behavior management and punishment) are best at changing behavior quickly. However, punishment techniques actually discourage self-discipline, instead causing resentment and poor self-esteem (see chapter 10).

The full discipline gradient, with discipline techniques listed for each area, is shown on the next page. The gradient shows at a glance which techniques are better at teaching self-discipline, and which techniques are better at changing behavior quickly.

The Discipline Gradient

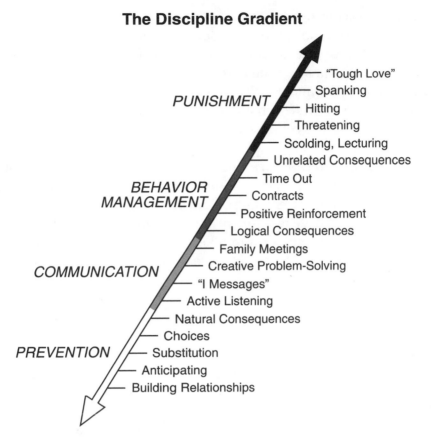

PUNISHMENT
- "Tough Love"
- Spanking
- Hitting
- Threatening
- Scolding, Lecturing
- Unrelated Consequences

BEHAVIOR MANAGEMENT
- Time Out
- Contracts
- Positive Reinforcement
- Logical Consequences

COMMUNICATION
- Family Meetings
- Creative Problem-Solving
- "I Messages"
- Active Listening

PREVENTION
- Natural Consequences
- Choices
- Substitution
- Anticipating
- Building Relationships

Prevention techniques often prevent a problem from occurring in the first place. Needless confrontations are damaging to the self-esteem of both child and parent as well as to the peace of the home. Prevention techniques require pre-thought on the parent's part, but are generally well worth the effort. These techniques are excellent at building children's decision-making skills and self-discipline.

Communication techniques open up channels of communication between parents and children to prevent or solve problems smoothly before they become repetitious or severe. These techniques are also very good at encouraging self-discipline. Both prevention and communication techniques help families tune in to each other and form loving relationships.

Behavior management techniques focus on changing a child's behavior. When problems become severe, relationships suffer. Simple, effective ways to change problem behaviors bring peace back to the family, leaving the way open to reestablish positive relationships and self-esteem. The strength of behavior management lies in quickly changing inappropriate behaviors. Behavior management techniques do not teach internal controls as well as those listed under prevention or communication.

Punishment techniques are on the gradient because many people use them, and because their position at the far end shows their relationship to the other techniques. Punishment relies on external control and tends to create resentment and rebellion. Chapter 10 discusses punishment and compares it to other discipline techniques. Punishment techniques may have influence at the time they are used, but they are poor at building internal controls.

As we move up the gradient from prevention to punishment, the techniques become less effective at establishing self-discipline. Internal controls are best built before problems become severe. A severe problem drives a wedge between parent and child and the relationship begins to suffer. In this case it may be better to work at changing the behavior first, then work backward on the gradient to rebuild relationships and communication.

The discipline techniques you choose to work on a particular problem will depend upon the following factors:
1. the severity of the problem,
2. to what extent you wish to teach internal controls,
3. your own preferences, what feels right to you,
4. your child's personality, likes and dislikes, and
5. the relationship between you and your child.

The severity of the problem

Often parents are troubled by problems that seem overwhelming, but that shrink in importance when compared to more severe concerns. In my classes, I have asked parents to rank problems in order of severity, or place them on a scale of 1 to 10. Where would you place "not going to bed at night" or "talking back to a parent" on a scale of 1 to 10? Where would you place "cheating on a test" or "an empty beer bottle found in a twelve-year-old's closet?"

If your answers were high—that is, above 8—consider how you would label running away from home, consistently skipping school, or driving under the influence of alcohol. What about shoplifting, purse snatching, or other robbery to pay for drug use?

The purpose of this exercise is to place child behaviors in perspective and to encourage the use of discipline techniques found under the prevention and communication sections of the gradient. Many developmental problems, even though consistent and annoying, can be handled satisfactorily for both parent and child by prevention or communication techniques.

For example, three-year-old Sarah, who has a two-month-old baby sister, refuses to go to bed at night when her parents ask her. She delays and whines nearly every night, often accusing her parents of wanting to be rid of her. Sarah's parents have tried pleading, threatening, bribing, spanking, and letting her stay up. Nothing works satisfactorily. To Sarah's parents this is a serious problem, warranting serious efforts to resolve it.

However, after considering the various techniques on the gradient, Sarah's parents decide to combine several prevention techniques, including *anticipating* the difficult transition time and easing it with a comforting routine, giving Sarah appropriate personal power through *choices*, and spending more time with Sarah at other times *(building relationships)*. Since going to bed at night is a common developmental problem (complicated by having to share attention with a new sibling), Sarah will probably respond well to the prevention techniques. In addition, these techniques will help Sarah build internal controls and will encourage a positive relationship between her and her parents.

Sarah's parents could have chosen a behavior management technique, such as a *star chart*, to approach this problem. Perhaps Sarah enjoys earning stickers and saving them for a special activity with Mom or Dad. A good reason for choosing a behaviorist technique would be if Sarah did not respond well to prevention or communication techniques. As problems become more severe, a parent may need to move up the gradient to find techniques that will work well. Behavior management techniques are often the best at changing difficult, repetitive behaviors. Since behavior management techniques are *less* effective at teaching internal controls, I encourage parents to combine these techniques with others closer to the beginning of the gradient. Sarah's parents could also have tried communication techniques: *active listening* (to encourage Sarah to share her feelings about the new baby) or *"I messages"* (explaining how the parents feel about the situation).

When Mrs. Jones (a single parent) found an empty beer bottle in twelve-year-old Josh's bedroom closet, her reaction was a combination of fear that Josh was drinking, fear that peer pressure was more influential than parental values, and hurt that he had betrayed her by drinking behind her back. She might have confronted him angrily, lectured him on the evils of alcohol and disobedience, and grounded him for a month. Instead, Mrs. Jones decided to try a combination of "I messages" and active listening—explaining her values and concerns, and actively listening to Josh's explanations, reasoning and feelings.

In this case, the communication between Josh and his mother aired the hurt, the fears, and Josh's concerns about being accepted by his friends. And, very importantly, it deepened the relationship between Josh and his mother.

However, a month later Mrs. Jones found a six-pack of beer in the garage. It was time to move up the gradient to a stronger technique. She decided to try a *contract* with Josh.

Teaching internal controls

Most parents will quickly agree that teaching self-discipline to their children is of primary importance. However, it takes time and forethought to choose and practice techniques that are good teachers of internal controls. In today's busy world, it is easier to react to a situation than to plan for it in advance.

Planning ahead, despite the extra time and effort, has several important advantages. First, the parents have time to consider the situation and their goals for their child, and to choose a technique they feel will be best for their child and family. Second, it is easier to discipline when we have thought things out in advance—anger is less likely to distort our perspective and make us say or do things we wish we hadn't. We also lose the feeling of helplessness that comes with our children's misbehavior, since we have planned a course of action and are now ready to implement it.

To help you plan in advance for discipline situations, the various techniques in this book are explained in detail with "how to" sections. In addition, exercises accompany each explanation to allow practice using each technique. Personal exercises are geared to help individualize a technique for your own home.

Your own preferences; what feels right to you

Ever since child rearing became a science, people of various schools of thought have tried to convince us that their philosophy of parenting is the best. In the discipline classes I teach, some parents eagerly reach out to try a specific technique, and others find it is just not for them. Or a parent may successfully use a technique with one child but find it doesn't work at all with his sibling.

One of the values of using the discipline gradient is that there are many techniques to choose from. If one technique does not work for you, there are others to try. I, like many of the parents who have taken our classes, have my favorite discipline techniques. In this book, I list many advantages of some very useful techniques, and hope that you will practice and experiment with them. However, the final decision about which discipline techniques to use in your family will be a personal one.

Your child's personality, likes and dislikes

Before my children were born, I listened to parents at supermarkets count to 3 (or 5, or 10) before the Great Consequence (whatever it was) was imposed. I thought smugly to myself, "At least that's one thing I will never do to my children."

You've guessed it. My first child, like most children, had a very difficult time responding quickly to a parental demand. Counting to 3 gave her a chance to assimilate the command, decide whether or not to follow it, and still have time to carry out my wishes before the Great Consequence. In this case, my daughter's personality (and not my preference) dictated which technique I chose to use.

My second daughter, however, did *not* respond well to the same technique. Upon hearing "1, 2, . . . 3," Jamie's heels dug into the carpet and she braced herself for confrontation. I quickly discovered that, no matter how inconvenient, we usually saved time and much hassle if I could creatively entice Jamie to do on her own what I wanted her to do.

Our children's personalities definitely play a part in our discipline choices. Some children are crushed by a reproving look or a raised voice. Others take up the challenge with great energy. Still others don't seem to notice our demands (certainly not our requests). In the following pages, I discuss which age child responds most readily to each discipline technique. But it is important to take into account your child's individual characteristics, as well as age.

The relationship between you and your child

Any discipline technique a parent uses will influence family relationships. Prevention and communication techniques tend to enrich relationships and create positive self-esteem for both parent and child. Behavior management techniques, although they do not directly enrich relationships as well as the first two categories, often positively influence those relationships by changing stressful behaviors. Punishment techniques usually weaken parent-child relationships.

The techniques listed on the gradient are not the only discipline techniques parents can use. However, most of these techniques have been used over a long period of time by many people, and show positive and effective results. The following chapters explain the various techniques, including when and how they may be used, the ages of children who respond well to them, advantages and disadvantages, and samples and worksheets for practice.

The best way to use the gradient in this book to help resolve discipline problems is to read about the different techniques and to work the exercises included with each section. By focusing on solutions rather than specific problems, our brains often come up with new, creative ways to approach issues. The "Practical" exercises give examples and practice in using the discipline techniques. The "Personal" exercises will help you decide how a particular technique would be useful for you.

Chapter 4

Prevention: Building Relationships and Anticipating

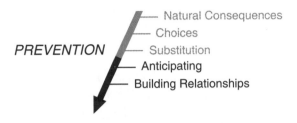

PREVENTION
— Natural Consequences
— Choices
— Substitution
— Anticipating
— Building Relationships

Skills that prevent problems and build positive self-esteem are first on the discipline gradient. Prevention techniques help a child learn internal controls. These techniques can defuse a potential conflict before it becomes a problem. When used with other techniques on the discipline gradient, prevention techniques communicate respect for the child and encourage self-discipline while shaping behaviors.

Establishing a positive relationship with your child is the first, fundamental "technique" of discipline. Other prevention techniques are anticipating (including preparing children for events, restructuring time, reducing boredom, and changing the environment), substitution, choices and natural consequences.

Building Positive Relationships

Limit-setting and enforcement does not work very well if you haven't established mutual liking and respect. One substitute teacher described her experience:

> "I began the morning as the first grade's substitute teacher by firmly laying down the rules. But this class, knowing my reign was temporary (and perhaps too young to fear consequences from

their regular teacher), ignored my strict manner. They didn't like me, so they would give me as rough a time as possible, and they proceeded to do so. After a very long day, I shuffled home to think out what I had done wrong.

"I realized that establishing a pleasant, respectful relationship with a class was even more fundamental than rule-setting. Without a positive relationship, enforcing the rules was an unpleasant struggle for power. But if the students respected me—even liked me—they were willing to do as I asked."

Nourishing positive relationships with your children tends to prevent discipline problems. Children want to please parents they love and respect. Discipline becomes a tool to learn together, grow together and build self-esteem. On the other hand, parents who do not have the time to put into relationships will find themselves drifting apart from their children. And discipline will become a harder and harder problem to solve.

In some ways developing relationships is the easiest discipline technique, since nurturing our children feels natural and right. But in other ways this is a difficult technique, because it requires what we never seem to have enough of—time and patience.

Building Relationships

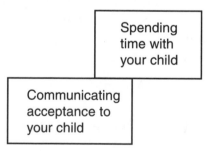

■ How to use this technique

Two main activities encourage a warm relationship between parent and child: communicating to the child your acceptance of who she is, and spending time with her.

Communicate your acceptance of your child. No matter how much we love our children, it will not directly encourage positive self-esteem unless we *communicate* that love. A child believes what she perceives—if she does not see evidence of love, she may very well believe it does not exist. If she perceives evidence of love and acceptance (such as personal attention), she is much more likely to believe that she is loved and that she is worthy of being loved.

All types of verbal and nonverbal nurturing are ideal for communicating acceptance. (See chapter 2 for more explanation and examples of nurturing.)

Sometimes acceptance is communicated by not intervening in a child's activities. A preschooler may be absorbed in a tea party with her dolls, stuffed animals and the friend next door. Refraining from interrupting gives them permission to develop their creative play as far as they want to take it.

At other times, communicating acceptance means being willing to be interrupted. Toddlers are often able to play by themselves for short periods, provided they can run to mom or dad for a quick moment of attention and reassurance before returning to their activities.

Listening communicates acceptance. Listening means stopping our activity to look at, listen to and respond to our child. Saying "that's nice" while making dinner or watching television does not communicate acceptance, but rather gives that sad feeling of "what mom or dad is doing is more important than I am." Listening requires verbal responses that encourage the child to talk more. Listening means refraining from interpreting, criticizing or giving advice. (See chapter 6 for more on listening skills.)

Perhaps the hardest time to communicate acceptance of a child is when we wish to change something about her. This is when the premise "separate the child from the behavior" is very helpful. When you need to offer discipline or criticism, be sure the child realizes you are criticizing *her behavior*, not the child herself. Don't reject the child because she hit her brother, because her room is messy or because she cheated on a test. Self-esteem comes from knowing someone cares about us, even when we did something wrong. *Especially* when we did something wrong.

Instead of rejecting the child:
"Bad boy!"

Confront the behavior directly:
"Hitting hurts!

Instead of accusing the child:
"How could you be so rude to Mrs. White?"

Confront the behavior directly:
"Saying something unkind about a person hurts their feelings."

A child's personality or habits may not mold into what the parent desires. How do we communicate acceptance if we don't feel it? The answer is: we cannot. Phony acceptance is easily recognized and rejected. In this case, the parent needs to take a good look at what he dislikes about the child:

Is it an attitude or behavior that is inappropriate for the situation or against the parents' morals? Inappropriate behaviors, especially dangerous ones, should not be ignored. For the health and happiness of child and family, explore reasons why the behavior is occurring and take steps to resolve the problem.

Is it a personality characteristic that would be difficult or uncomfortable for the child to change? (For example, witty comments that make others laugh but the parent cringe? only-average grades?) Real acceptance means accepting all of a child's characteristics, even though some are less preferred than others. When a child does not meet an expectation, parents can (a) allow the disappointment or hurt to come between parent and child, (b) push for change, accepting the risk that the child may rebel or unhappily acquiesce, or (c) let go of the disappointment or hurt, accept that the child is different, and enjoy and encourage the parent-child relationship. It is much healthier for your child's development and for your mutual relationship if you are able to relax perfectionism and allow your child to be who she is.

Spend time alone with your child. Children's early self-esteem is based on their perception of their parents' love and acceptance. Children measure that love by the amount and quality of attention they receive from a parent.

Spending family time with your children builds rewarding relationships among all family members. Children get practice in sharing, in decision-making and problem-solving, in learning new activities and in enjoying people in a group.

One of the best ways to communicate acceptance and build warm relationships is to spend time alone with your child every day. This may seem impossible, especially if both parents work or have more than one child. However, taking time to nourish the individual bonds between you and your children will actually save time later—time you might have spent resolving discipline problems. Dr. T. Berry Brazelton, a leader in the field of parent-child relationships, suggests spending at least an hour alone with each child per week. Spending time alone with your child shows her that she is important to you.

How do you find time to go somewhere alone with a child? I used to plan special outings with my middle child, but a needy baby and a preschooler (plus work and husband) somehow postponed them. When two-and-a-half-year-old Jamie began sulking or engaging in other inappropriate behaviors, I would drop everything and arrange an outing for the two of us. Her attitude and behaviors would change like magic.

I realized I needed to find special time for Jamie more often. Instead of planning a big outing, I looked for short but frequent opportunities during the day. Jamie tended to take long naps and have a hard time waking up. I would crawl into bed with her after her nap, snuggle a little, talk a little, sometimes tell a story or sing a song. We both enjoyed these interludes, and the other children never missed us for those few minutes each day.

As Jamie grew older, it was still difficult to arrange special outings. But we found time to do chores together—especially fun ones like making cookies, exercising or painting. The activity itself seemed less important than the fact that we did it together, taking pleasure in each other's company.

One mother with five teenagers found time to be alone with each one (in the car) by arranging to drive to school activities and by stopping with one teen for a fast-food lunch or late-night coffee after a school event. Another favorite way to be alone with her teens was to grab the evening paper and hide away in one teen's room. Throwing herself on a daughter's bed, the mother would exclaim, "Can I hide in here for a little to escape the noise?" Sometimes they would read quietly together, but often mother and teen found themselves in rewarding conversation.

■ Why is this technique valuable?

Positive relationships between family members are the rewards of parenthood. You will also be modeling to your child how relationships develop and are nurtured.

But in addition, you are giving your child some of the greatest gifts you are able to give—your attention, your concern, your love, your guidance. These are the seeds of self-esteem. Children with positive self-images tend to grow into happy, fulfilled adults who are able to relate well to others. One of the most important factors in your child's self-esteem is the relationship he has with you, his parents. The first ideas of self-esteem and relationships are learned at home.

Children who like and respect their parents—as well as love them—want to please their parents. Those children who do not feel a warm bond with their parents tend to test limits more, rebel more, have more resentment and less commitment than children who do feel such bonds. A strong parent-child relationship will encourage mutual problem solving and self-discipline.

■ Cautions

"Quality time" is sometimes overplanned by a parent. Sanger and Kelly, in *The Woman Who Works, The Parent Who Cares*, suggest taking cues from the child when spending time together. Jason may not be that excited about the paint, the clay and the model ship that his dad has chosen for tonight's activity. He may be more interested in hearing again the same old favorite bedtime story, with time out for snuggles and a quiet conversation. Or perhaps he is deeply involved in coloring and doesn't share his father's desire to move on to the woodworking project. Taking the cue from the child, Jason's dad will use the activity to further the relationship, instead of using the allotted time to finish the activity.

■ When to use this technique

Special outings with one parent and one child are a great way to spend individual time together. Choose an activity that your child particularly enjoys, or better yet, let your child participate in the choice. Take your child out to lunch, go swimming together, walk in the park, build a snowman. Outings need not be expensive.

But don't depend on outings for individual time with your children. Shorter shared times can happen during any spare moment of the day. Involve your children in your activities. Children who help parents with indoor and outdoor chores are learning about responsibility as well as about relationships. Take advantage of opportunities when your child invites you to play with him. Special time with a parent before bedtime can help a child settle down from the day's activities, protest less about going to bed, and fall asleep with the flush of love and attention in his heart.

Take your cue from your child. Don't rush in to create quality time when your child is involved in her own activity. Try not to allow your special time with your child to be shadowed by a pressing worry or deadline.

■ Ages of children

Working at establishing a warm relationship with your child is valuable throughout your child's lifetime: in infancy, when the baby looks to you for fulfillment of basic needs, warmth and touch; with toddlers, who need safety and guidance; with preschoolers and school-age children, who are exploring and expanding their skills and self-image; with teens, who are looking away from the family but still want and need you to be there for them; even with adult children, who are building adult friendships with their parents.

Parents are concerned about bonding with newborn infants—which is indeed important—but sometimes we take for granted our relationships with older children. In order to grow stronger, relationships must be encouraged, not neglected. Establishing and enriching the parent-child relationship is one of the fundamental tasks of parenting.

EXERCISES
Building Positive Relationships

Practical Exercise

How would you communicate acceptance:

1. to your unwed teen daughter after she tells you she is pregnant?

2. to your teenage son who was just selected for the state's honor band?

3. to Tammy who is falling behind in the class you teach?

4. to three-year-old Cameron who just built a snowman?

5. to Kenny whose voice is changing?

How could Kristi find time to spend alone with each of the children in the family described below?

Kristi is a single mother with three children: thirteen-year-old Louis, nine-year-old Zachary and three-year-old Sally. Kristi works from 9 to 5 weekly and earns just enough to support the family. She spends evenings during the week making dinner, doing dishes, yelling at Louis and Zachary to do their homework, collapsing for an hour-long television show, and reading Sally a bedtime story. On Saturdays, Kristi does the housekeeping, shopping and laundry. On Sundays, the family sleeps in, the kids watch television or visit friends, and Kristi makes a big family meal. Sometimes the whole family goes out to a movie or some other outing. Sally's daycare center is two blocks from Kristi's work. Louis and Zachary walk to school in the morning, leaving about 8:30 a.m. Louis plays soccer twice weekly from 3:30 to

5 p.m. (a neighbor drives him). Zachary loves books and spends most of his free time reading. The children's father lives in the same city and takes all three children every other weekend.

Personal Exercise

1. What activities does your child particularly enjoy?

2. What activities do you particularly enjoy?

3. What activities do you do together with your child? Which ones do you enjoy? Are there any you don't enjoy? Why not?

4. What would you like to do with your child if you had the time?

5. What outings do you (or your partner) take with each child individually?

6. What characteristics does your child have that are hard to accept?

7. How do you show your child that you love him/her?

Anticipating

Every discipline situation centers on one or more needs—the child's, the parent's, or both. Anticipating needs and working to fulfill them in advance can prevent problems from arising. If Mom knows that Nathan becomes irritable when he is tired, she is wise not to take him with her to an important meeting before naptime. If Dad has a hard time after work jumping in to play with the kids before he reads the newspaper, he might consider reading the paper before leaving work.

Transitions are times when one activity is ending and the next is about to begin. Daily transitions for children include beginning and finishing meals, falling asleep and waking up, preparing to leave the house, or returning home after a long day. Larger transitions include moving between homes in shared custody situations, going on vacation, returning to school in the fall or moving to a new neighborhood. Transitions are difficult times for all ages, but particularly for young children. By anticipating the extra stress of transitions, parents can plan ways to avoid problems during these times.

Anticipating takes preparation, but it saves time and frustration by defusing a problem before it starts. Most anticipating strategies are common sense. However, in the crush of busy lives, parents often forget to anticipate and are left dealing with unplanned situations.

Four different anticipating techniques help prevent discipline situations before they occur: preparing children for events, restructuring time, reducing boredom and changing the environment.

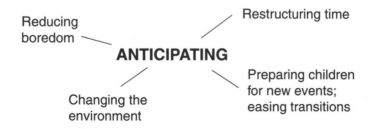

Anticipating by preparing children for events

Knowing in advance what is expected can turn a frightening experience into an adventure, and can help a child make behavioral choices most appropriate for the situation.

■ How to use this technique

1. Prepare a child for a new event by explaining it before it happens. Talking about the arrival and visit of an unknown relative can prepare a child for having this stranger in his home (perhaps using his room). Show him a picture of the relative; say how long she will be staying and where the child will sleep during the visit.

Discussing a trip to the doctor or the first day of school can help the child deal with the unknown situation. Another way to prepare a child is to read a book together about a corresponding situation. You can find children's books today on many topics such as going to the dentist or the doctor, the first day of school, making friends, or divorce.

2. Warn the child in advance that a transition is about to occur. Warning a child that something new is about to happen gives him a few minutes to readjust his thinking and be more willing to change. It is difficult to stop in the middle of something, especially if you are enjoying yourself.

Examples:
"We need to leave in 15 minutes. Why don't you each take one more turn on the swings, and then it will be time to go."

(in the car) "We'll be home in a few minutes. When we get in the house, you can play in the sunroom until I have the groceries put away and it's time for lunch."

3. Use rituals to smooth transitions. Rituals are repeated actions surrounding an event. Bedtime rituals—such as bath, pajamas, brushing teeth, reading a story—are very effective in helping a child separate from activity. It is difficult for a child to move directly from playing a game to falling asleep at night. But the transition is not quite so hard if the steps are smaller and flow logically. Once the sequence is started, habit and routine encourage the next step. When the child has made it through the bedtime story and the good-night snuggle, it is much easier for sleepy eyes to close than it would have been before the ritual began.

Rituals can be established for nearly any transition.

Examples:

(after school) Change out of school clothes, snack, homework, free time before dinner.

(coming back from dad's house) Each child unpacks his or her own suitcase, special dinner of pizza or other favorite food, family activity such as playing a game together.

(at a child-care center) Soft music indicates to children that it is time to put away toys, wash hands and be seated for lunch.

4. Prepare a child for a special event. A special event is any event that requires specific behavior on the part of the child. Make expectations clear. If you need to make an important business call, perhaps your toddler can go into another room to play, or your older child can watch him. If that is not possible, talk with the toddler before the call. Tell him how important it is to play quietly until the call is over. Bring out special toys.

If the event is a wedding, special party or other occasion, explain what will happen there and what behavior you expect from the child. Clearly communicated expectations can prevent discipline problems in situations away from the home.

■ Why is this technique valuable?

A child feels greater confidence when he knows in advance what things will happen in a new situation. When a child knows what is expected of him, there is less likelihood of mistakes in behavior and the resulting frustration for both parent and child.

Unnecessary power struggles take their toll on the parent-child relationship. Many problems can be eliminated if the parent thinks ahead.

■ Cautions

When preparing a child for a new event that might not be completely pleasant (such as going to the dentist), present a calm, confident air, but do not lie about or leave out unpleasant parts. Children need to trust that what you tell them is true, and they will not trust you in the future if you misrepresent something in order to get their cooperation in the present.

■ When to use this technique

Prepare children before new events they haven't experienced before, especially if they are scary or threatening. Even happy, exciting occasions (like going to the fair or to your first birthday party) can be scary to a child. What will happen? How should I act? What if something awful happens?

Prepare your child for transitions by giving an advance warning that the transition is about to occur. Use rituals at bedtime, at mealtimes, for getting ready in the morning and other transitions.

Prepare children for special events such as church functions, parties, job responsibilities or vacations. Making expectations clear in advance will help prevent undesirable behavior from the child who simply did not know what was expected of him.

■ Ages of children

New events: Preparing children for new events is helpful at all age levels. It is especially effective for younger children, for whom each new experience poses new questions and fears.

As children grow older, their background of past experiences gives them a basis for understanding new experiences. However, even teens can benefit from this technique. How about talking over the first job interview before it happens? The driver's test?

Transitions: Warn young children right before a transition. Warn older children several days, or even weeks, before a larger transition such as back to school, vacations or special outings. Even teens and adults appreciate some warning before quick transitions ("We have to leave in 15 minutes") and before special events ("Your aunt's wedding is two weeks away. Should we plan your dress now?")

Special events: Children of all ages, including teens, benefit from preparation for important events. Young children need to have expectations made clear right before the event—even if discussed previously—because they forget rules quickly. Reminders before the rules are broken will avoid frustration and disappointment.

EXERCISES

Preparing Children for Events

Practical Exercise

New events: how can you prepare your child for:
1. her first birthday party?

2. a long plane ride?

3. the first time overnight with a friend?

4. her first date?

Transitions: how can you help your child move smoothly from one activity to the next?
1. *from* playing at a friend's house *to* going home

2. *from* watching television *to* going to bed

3. *from* sleeping *to* getting up and getting ready for school

4. *from* living at mom's house *to* going to dad's house for the summer

Personal Exercise

Can you defuse the problem before it starts?

1. Describe the discipline problem:

2. When does the behavior occur—at what particular times, places, and with what people present? How often does it occur?

3. Consider your child's developmental stage. Is the problem a common one for your child's age?

4. Whose needs are not being met?

5. What could you do to help meet everyone's needs *before* the problem behavior arises?

6. What transitions are particularly difficult for you and your child?

7. How can you make the transitions in #6 easier for all?

Anticipating by restructuring time

Certain times of the day are particularly stressful, usually when several people are trying to meet their needs simultaneously. Sara wants to zip her coat herself and find exactly the right toy to take with her. Sara's mother wants to get to an appointment on time. Older brother Tim wants to be sure to get the window seat in the car. Ordinarily these are not large problems, but taken together, tempers rise and patience disappears. Readjusting the sequence of events can sometimes reduce tension and prevent inappropriate behaviors.

■ How to use this technique

Consider a stressful time of day. Rearrange the sequence of events to make things flow more easily during that time. Think about the needs of the people involved. What makes the situation stressful? Whose needs are not being met? How can those needs be met in a different way or at a different time?

In the example above, Mom and Sara could choose her toy the night before. Mom and Tim could discuss earlier whose turn it was to sit by the window. It might be possible to simply schedule the appointment for a later time, or to get up earlier to get the children ready.

Other examples of restructuring time:
- Allowing a young child to sleep in comfortable clothes (rather than pajamas) to minimize the early morning hassle of dressing for daycare.
- Making and freezing dinners on weekends to bake on weeknights, if both parents work during the week.
- Grocery shopping early in the morning or later in the evening to avoid crowds.
- Filling up the gas tank in the car before it gets so low that it becomes an emergency.
- Collecting all the homework, library books and lunch money for school on the evening before; helping children choose and lay out their clothes.
- Creating a fictitious deadline for a business report which is actually a day or more before the real deadline. This gives you an added cushion for completing an important project.

- Doing the heavy cleaning and major baking a day or two before the big party, saving the party day for last-minute touches or reassuring excited children.
- For important instructions or other communication, choosing times that are convenient for the listener, as well as the speaker. Don't try to discuss an important conflict right before a favorite television show or before a teen leaves on a date.

■ Why is this technique valuable?

Any time we minimize stress, we decrease the chances of impatience, anger and inappropriate behaviors. Taking a few minutes in advance to rearrange a situation can save a lot of time and temper in the long run. It is not always possible to add time to a person's schedule, but activities could be arranged earlier or later so the scheduled time is not so hectic.

■ Cautions

Determine your priorities. Do you really want to get as much done in as fast a time as possible? Having a younger child help you do the dishes or fold the laundry may initially take more time. However, being able to teach your child responsibilities and skills—as well as his enjoyment of being included—may outweigh the fact that you could do it yourself with less time and hassle.

■ When to use this technique

Restructure time whenever it will defuse potential discipline situations, particularly during transitions. Write down the most stressful times of the day, the week and the month for your family. Then jot down ideas to rearrange activities during those times.

■ Ages of children

Restructuring time can be used for all ages, including adults trying to fulfill their own needs. It is particularly useful with young children.

EXERCISES

Restructuring Time

Practical Exercise

What activities can be restructured to help reduce conflict in the situation below?

The Witter family has a rough time between 4:30 and 6 p.m. Sean, age 9, returns from school hungry and tired and wants Mom's attention. Jesse, 8 months, gets fussy and wants to be fed and comforted. Dad comes home from work and wants a few minutes to relax. Mom—who works two days weekly—tries to fix dinner.

Personal Exercise

1. Describe your most frustrating time of day. What activity is each person (yourself, partner, children) involved in during that time?

2. Whose needs are not being met?

3. How can you restructure activities or timing to meet everyone's needs during that time?

4. Are there any rituals that could help ease tensions and provide activities during transition times?

Anticipating by reducing boredom

Idle hands are more likely to produce inappropriate behaviors. When you have an activity planned that requires the children's special cooperation, it is a good idea to have on hand enough distractions to defeat boredom, with its corresponding discipline problems.

■ How to use this technique

Most infants and toddlers—and even preschoolers or school-age children—find it difficult to wait patiently for a long time, such as in a doctor's waiting room or during a church service. In such situations, quiet activities or toys help hold the child's attention and prevent the noisy outbreaks we'd rather avoid.

If young children are bored while you are doing housework or other chores, give them a small part of the job as their responsibility. They will enjoy working with you and will begin learning skills.

Save a grocery bag on a kitchen shelf. During the week, put in unwanted household items and bring them out when boredom strikes. Egg cartons, junk mail, empty spools, fabric scraps and old magazines are great inexpensive toys for toddlers and preschoolers.

When traveling, especially on long car or plane trips, pack goody bags of inexpensive toys or magazines. Something new every hour is a nice surprise that makes the trip shorter. Toddlers and preschoolers will enjoy many common household items to sort and stretch—like Band-Aids, rubber bands, tape measure, magnets—which also have the advantage of being small for airline packing. Inexpensive toys sold in grocery stores can be bought ahead of time and saved for the trip.

Put away some toys at home and bring them out when parents need quiet time, during long-distance phone calls, or when you have to finish a report without interruptions. Most children have a wide variety of toys sitting on shelves that they don't play with as much as we think they should. Use this variety to your advantage. Rotate toys. Keep available some standards like puzzles and building blocks, but put others away to be forgotten for a rainy day.

Does your child have many toys, but they are all scattered around her room or thrown into one big box? It's not too much fun to play with puzzles, games, doll clothes or building sets that have pieces missing. The parent can encourage organization and provide boxes or shelves to keep toys attractively arranged. Ask the child to do her share of keeping pieces where they belong.

Is your child a chronic complainer? Does she watch a lot of television? Watching television is a passive activity. Children get used to being entertained. Then when the television is turned off, they want someone else to entertain them. Parents need to encourage active participation—not just outdoor activities, which are certainly valuable, but creative activities such as pretend games, arts and crafts. Children benefit from figuring out ideas to entertain themselves. Because television offers an audiovisual feast, a child is not required to imagine in the same way as when she reads a book or hears a story. Too much television discourages creativity and imagination. It is much easier for the child to feel bored.

Preschoolers and school-age children benefit from availability of toys, lessons and group activities. Large blocks of unsupervised time can lead to trouble. A balance of structured and unstructured activities allows development of imagination and creativity. As children grow older, having a friend over or going over to a friend's house is a good way to reduce boredom, as well as an excellent way to promote social skills and encourage relationships.

■ Why is this technique valuable?

Discipline problems often arise when children are bored. Eliminating the boredom eliminates the problem and saves wear and tear on relationships.

■ Cautions

Chronic complaining of boredom requires a closer look at the situation. Besides the hints above about rotating toys and watching too much television, check into any special stress or problems your child may be experiencing. Does she have a new teacher at school? Has her best friend moved away? Have mom and dad been extra busy lately?

Children may complain of one problem (boredom), but actually may be missing or needing something else (extra attention or help).

On a lighter note, if you are fairly sure your child is not particularly troubled, but she still complains of boredom, you can always offer her a choice of chores to do.

■ When to use this technique

Plan ahead to eliminate boredom on trips, during waiting times such as doctor's appointments, or whenever the parent is occupied (e.g., phone calls, visitors, work deadlines).

Rotate toys every few months. Toys suddenly assume a new attractiveness after they have disappeared for a time.

When school is out for the summer or for holidays, be aware of your children's activities and provide a variety of things to do, friends to visit or outings to take. Vacations are often a challenge because students have become used to strictly scheduled time, and they may find it overwhelming to have an unstructured expanse of time ahead of them. Help them make lists of activities they like; provide some structure to ease them into the holiday, but also encourage them to discover their own daily activities.

■ Ages of children

Anticipating by reducing boredom is most helpful for babies, toddlers and preschoolers. School-age children also benefit from planning for idle times.

The idea can be adapted for older children and teens. A teen with lots of time on her hands can be encouraged to take a part-time job, participate in group activities, take lessons, learn a hobby or become active in volunteer work.

EXERCISES

Reducing Boredom

Practical Exercise

What can you do to reduce boredom for the children in the following situations to help prevent discipline problems?

1. Mother is taking Melodie, age 3, to a doctor's appointment at 2 p.m. There is often a long waiting time.

2. Carol, age 11, is an only child. Her parents are planning a two-week camping trip for the family this summer.

3. Mother is trying to finish a sewing project. Timmy, age 2, keeps interrupting her.

4. Ken, age 9, and Tammy, age 7, are bored with their books while traveling in the car. The trip is three hours long.

5. Janet, age 5, is accompanying her father on a daylong business outing to a construction site.

6. Elizabeth, age 10, and Skye, age 14, will be spending the summer at home while their parents work.

7. Steven, age 6, has to wait for an hour and a half each week while his sisters take violin lessons.

8. Demetri, age 4, comes along with his mother to a quilters' meeting for two hours each Tuesday evening.

Personal Exercise

1. How many hours per day does your child watch television?

2. When (what time of day) does your child watch television?

3. When would you prefer your child to watch television? How many hours per day? What shows?

4. Are your child's toys, books and art supplies arranged in an orderly and attractive way?

5. How could toys be better arranged for easy access and organization?

6. What toys could be put away for a rainy day? Which toys could be rotated?

7. Describe a situation that causes your child to feel bored.

8. How can you reduce that boredom?

Reducing Boredom

Anticipating by changing the environment

A parent in one of my classes brought up a situation that was extremely frustrating to her, her husband and their three-year-old daughter. "Kerry keeps trying to climb up the ladder to the roof where my husband is working. I've tried saying 'no' firmly; I've tried explaining the danger; I've tried consequences," said the mother. "I just can't keep Kerry off the ladder!"

"Why don't you put a board up across the first few steps so she can't climb up?" asked another parent in the class.

Kerry's parents tried the suggestion and brought us the results in the next class meeting. "It works!" said Kerry's mother. "And best of all, it saves all the arguing and frustration."

■ How to use this technique

Change the environment around the child to eliminate safety hazards or potential discipline problems. Changing the environment does not always mean taking away—it may mean adding something. For example, keep an attractive bowl of raw vegetables in the refrigerator to encourage nutritious snacks.

Babyproofing one's home is the process of putting out of reach anything dangerous or undesirable for a baby or toddler. Constantly saying "no" is wearying for both parent and child. Why not eliminate the problem by putting a few things away until the child is older? Babies and toddlers need a few, firm limits, primarily around safety issues. Constant confrontations weaken the parent-child relationship.

Examples of changing the environment for babies and toddlers:
- Placing breakable items out of reach.
- Locking away medicines and matches.
- Using babyproof locks on cabinets and drawers.
- Guarding against scissors and knives left on the edges of tables and countertops, where they could be reached by a baby or toddler.
- Putting plants in hanging pots. Becoming knowledgeable about which plants have poisonous leaves or flowers, and eliminating these from your home or placing them well out of reach.
- Not allowing juice in a room with a light carpet.
- Arranging furniture or gates to limit access to stairs.

- Setting aside the lowest bookshelf for your child's books.
- Bolting tall bookshelves to walls.
- Putting second-best photos in an album for your child's use, to look at when you are working with your own photos.
- Having a toy piano for your baby or toddler to play when you want to practice on your own piano.
- Checking tables and other furniture to make sure legs are spaced far enough apart or close enough together so a baby's head would not get stuck between.
- Keeping a kitchen cabinet of unbreakable dishes or pots for little hands to play with while you are cooking.
- Storing juice and milk in smaller containers for little hands to practice pouring (and save demands on parents).

For older children:
- Providing places to play, to do homework and to store larger play equipment such as skis and bicycles.
- Keeping often-used child materials (art supplies, books, healthy snacks) in a place easy to reach.
- Providing clothes baskets or hampers for different colors of laundry.
- Letting your children (and spouse) sort their soiled clothes, saving time before washing.
- Storing extra toilet tissue, paper towels and facial tissues where they can be easily reached. (Teach your children to get a new box or roll whenever the old one is depleted.)
- Keeping an extra jar of pencils for kids. (Put away items that get borrowed and not returned—keys, sunglasses, stapler—or buy extras.)

■ Why is this technique valuable?

Many problems can be avoided simply by changing the environment around the child.

Although some parents feel that small children should learn not to touch, babyproofing is becoming more and more popular. There are several important advantages: (a) dangerous substances are locked away and not available for the odd moment when the parent's attention is occupied elsewhere, or when a babysitter is supervising, (b) unnecessary "no's" are avoided, which drain energy and cause frustration to both parents and child, (c) the child does not feel constantly restrained, but is encouraged to explore her environment—which allows the child to be curious and outgoing (less passive) as she grows.

■ Cautions

Knowing your house is child-proofed does not ensure your child's safety. A guest or another family member may have dropped a coin or pin which would be dangerous to your baby. A child may discover how to climb bookshelves or dresser bureaus. However, a child-proofed house does limit dangers, giving you more time to enjoy your child.

Many common household items that are not thought of as dangerous—such as toothpaste, hand lotion, perfume, dish soap—cause accidental poisonings and deaths each year.

■ When to use this technique

Whenever the environment can be changed to make the situation less stressful.

■ Ages of children

Babyproofing is for infants and toddlers.

Other environmental changes can be helpful for older children, such as not having candy in the house if you don't want children to eat it; keeping firearms locked away; or putting away mail, papers and projects so they are not accidentally lost or destroyed.

EXERCISES
Changing the Environment

Practical Exercise

How would you change the environment to prevent the following situations?

1. Peter, two years old, keeps pulling the cat's tail.

2. Three-year-old Jerry whines for mom or dad to wash him up after meals because he can't turn on the water faucet by himself.

3. Mom and Dad want to sleep late on Saturdays, but their two- and four-year-old sons always wake them up early to get breakfast.

4. Gary, age 12, wants to play the stereo after school, but his sister Gwen, age 9, can't hear the television.

5. Jack, four years old, keeps taking his older sister's art supplies.

Personal Exercise

Describe a situation with your child that might be modified by changing the environment.

1. What is the undesirable behavior?

2. How could you change the environment to prevent the problem?

Chapter 5

Prevention: Substitution, Choices and Natural Consequences

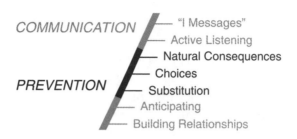

COMMUNICATION
— "I Messages"
— Active Listening
— Natural Consequences
— Choices
PREVENTION
— Substitution
— Anticipating
— Building Relationships

Substitution

Disappointment causes a baby to cry louder, and a child to complain or whine harder. Substitution helps eliminate or reduce disappointment by replacing a disputed object with a more appropriate object, or by replacing a canceled event with an alternative activity.

▉ How to use this technique

For babies and toddlers: Babies grab and chew to learn about their environments. If the baby is chewing your expensive bracelet or this month's bills, provide a substitute when you take away the inappropriate item. If the toddler is teasing the older children while they try to play Monopoly, give the toddler his own (indestructible) game to play with.

For any age: If a planned event falls through, choose an alternative event in its place. If the rain cancels your picnic, can you visit a museum instead, or have a smaller impromptu picnic on the living room floor? If the funds for the Disneyland vacation are eaten up in unexpected taxes, how about a shorter camping trip that will still be fun, and will soften the disappointment? If the family movie you intended to see was just changed to a new one you don't like, how about a family pizza and a home video?

▓ Why is this technique valuable?

For babies and toddlers: A baby doesn't understand why he can't eat lipstick or tear pages out of books. It is very upsetting when an adult stops an activity that is enjoyable (or has potential). By replacing the undesirable object or activity with a safer or less-expensive substitute, the baby can still enjoy his activity, chewing on a teething ring instead of lipstick, or ripping old catalogs instead of books. It is easier on mom or dad, too—fewer shrieks of unhappiness as the child adjusts to his loss.

For all ages: Whenever an anticipated event falls through, children (and also adults) are inevitably disappointed. An alternative event dispels some of that disappointment and cheers us up. Do we really need to mope around feeling awful because something we wanted didn't happen? Choosing an alternate activity is making the best of the situation—a good skill to learn.

▓ Cautions

Objects: When you see your small child with something he shouldn't have—especially if it is dangerous, like a knife or scissors—try not to shout or grab it away from him. If the object is dangerous, your quick or loud actions might frighten him into a sudden movement that could hurt him or someone else. Instead, speak calmly, hold out your hand and ask him to give you the knife—since it is dangerous and could hurt—and firmly offer a replacement toy. With this reaction, the child is more likely to give up the knife and accept the substitute. Even if he does not release the knife willingly, it gives you time to walk closer to him so you can take it away gently and firmly. Thank your child, even if he has not given up the object willingly. Besides the safety reasons, this ritual models important courtesies to your child—asking politely and thanking—rather than modeling the alternative, which is grabbing.

Activities: If you are not certain a special activity will occur, it is better to not mention it to your children until plans finalize. There are also risks to telling children about a planned event many days before it is scheduled. It is very hard for children to understand reasons why something has to be canceled. Even if the reason is ironclad—the birthday girl came down with chicken pox, the store went out of business—many times the child just doesn't understand why we couldn't fix it.

■ When to use this technique

Substitute a different object when you need to take away something dangerous or inappropriate from a baby or toddler.

Substitute a different activity when a planned or anticipated activity falls through.

■ Ages of children

Use substitution of objects with infants and toddlers. (Occasionally it may come in handy with older children.)

Use substitution of activities with children of all ages. Infants and toddlers may not understand why the promised activity did not occur, but they will still be cheered by an enjoyable alternate activity.

Substitution

For babies and toddlers: Provide a substitute when you take away an inappropriate item.
For any age: If a planned event falls through, choose an alternative event in its place.

EXERCISES

Substitution

Practical Exercise

How would you use substitution in the following examples?

1. Seven-month-old Jenny has triumphantly crawled over to her big sister's paper dolls and is about to start ripping.

2. Three-year-old Corey is stacking water glasses into a tower on the kitchen table.

3. Two-year-old Sam wants to copy Mom when she sews. He grabs her pincushion and pretends to sew with a needle.

4. Fifteen-year old Liana is marking up the kitchen calendar with homework deadlines.

What activities could you substitute for each of the following:

5. When you and your family arrive at the swimming pool, you unexpectedly find it is closed for cleaning.

6. The children's concert is sold out.

7. Mom plans to take the children biking in the country on Saturday, but she sprains her ankle on Friday.

Personal Exercise

1. Describe an undesirable behavior of your child that might be eliminated through substitution.

2. What similar, more appropriate object or activity could you substitute?

3. What events does your child eagerly look forward to?

4. What alternate activities could you substitute for each of the events in #3 above, if a long-awaited event had to be canceled?

Choices

In earlier times, people did not have the vast array of choices that face us today. Children followed in their father's footsteps, or followed social or economic limitations in selecting a school, job, mate or place to live. Today we can relocate to a different community, a different state or even a different country. Many new careers are available that didn't exist fifty years ago. Different schooling options are available for people from a wide variety of social and economic backgrounds.

At earlier and earlier ages today, children are faced with many decisions we parents may wish were not available. How can we help our children make choices about drug use, premarital sex, drinking and driving? A child who has not learned decision-making skills—a child who is used to being told what to do—will have trouble making his own decisions. He will follow, as he is used to following. But he may follow the desires of a peer group rather than a parent's wishes.

Decision-making skills are becoming a requirement in today's world. Offering choices to our children helps build those skills in the protected environment of the family. The earlier children begin making choices on their own, the longer they will have to practice and refine this extremely important skill. Solid decision-making skills—especially in a child with positive self-esteem—will prevent some tough discipline problems as the child grows older.

Choices can also be used directly as a discipline technique when used as a distraction, or when used in combination with consequences. This section discusses choices in discipline in each of three ways: (a) choices for their own sake, to help build decision-making skills, (b) distracting choices, and (c) choices used with consequences.

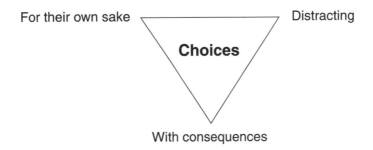

■ How to use this technique

1. Choices for their own sake. The opportunities for choices are endless. Toddlers can be offered limited choices about things that make little or no difference to parents. They can choose between two play outfits, between two snacks, between two activities. *Limited* choices are appropriate for most situations. Asking "What would you like to eat for dinner?" is asking for trouble. Surely your children, no matter what their ages, will ask for something not in the house or not appropriate (ice cream sundaes). Instead, offer two or three choices that are acceptable to you, the parent. "Would you like baked potatoes or rice with your chicken?"

As children grow older, choices increase. Preschool children might choose what friend they want to come over to play. School-age children might choose what school outfit to wear and what extracurricular activity they would like to try this semester. Teens, with guidance, could purchase their own clothing and choose their own classes, activities and friends.

Offering choices to a child of any age requires extra time and patience. It is easier to say "Here are your clothes; put them on," rather than "Which one do you want to wear today?" Children often have a difficult time making a decision. It takes extra time to wait for them to weigh all the alternatives and pick one. But the advantages of allowing choices are well worth the extra wait. As children become more familiar with the decision-making process, they will not only take less time to make routine decisions, but will eventually take over the less difficult decisions completely—saving you a lot of time, while building independence and confidence.

2. Distracting choices. In addition to developing decision-making skills, choices can be an excellent discipline tool. Distracting choices are used to distract a child from a major issue by offering a small related choice with appropriate power. When the toddler is upset about a situation—such as getting ready for bed or going to daycare—a simple choice can focus his attention on the *process,* instead of magnifying his resistance to the activity. "Would you like to wear your blue pajamas or your red pajamas?" "Would you like to put your coat on first or your boots on first?" Suddenly the child is busy making his choice—and happily exercising personal power—even though the big battle of going to bed or to daycare was not his to decide.

Use distracting choices primarily with young children. (Older children figure it out and it doesn't work any more.) Choose your strategy ahead of time, before the problem situation occurs. If Tony is consistently having trouble picking up his toys, try "Which do you want to pick up first, the blocks or the dishes?" Be willing, with a young child, to get down on the floor and help pick up. "Would you like me to put away the truck or the doll?"

3. *Choices combined with consequences.* When distracting choices do not work (with an older or strong-willed child), you can offer a consequence as a choice. "You may use my sewing kit and put it away afterward, or you may give up the right to use my sewing kit. You decide." "You may get up early so I can drive you, or you may walk to school." "You may play quietly in the house, or you may go outside to play. You choose." Offering a consequence as a choice is a great way to avoid getting angry. It puts the responsibility for the consequence on the child. In that way the parent is not perceived as the powerful punisher, and children learn that their actions have consequences (see "Logical Consequences," chapter 8).

▉ Why is this technique valuable?

Choices are placed close to the beginning of the gradient and listed under prevention because they teach internal controls and encourage positive parent-child relationships. Choices prevent discipline problems by encouraging responsibility, a sense of personal power and positive self-esteem. Choices can also be used specifically in a discipline confrontation by distracting a child from a power struggle or by offering a consequence as a choice.

Being able to make decisions and influence your own life increases positive self-esteem as you explore who you are and what you can do. Decision-making skills help children grow into independent people who are able to influence their environment. When children make appropriate choices, they exercise personal power in their lives and learn responsibility for their actions.

Teens are involved in the difficult process of moving away from their parents, looking toward their futures, and agonizing over endless little decisions in practice for bigger decisions ahead. *The best thing you can do for your teenager is to give him choices when he is a toddler.* Children who grow up making choices have a whole childhood of learning how to make appropriate decisions and accept responsibility. Everyone wins. The child builds a strong sense of self-esteem and learns skills to tackle the stormy teen years. The parents, who have spent eighteen years slowly allowing their child to become autonomous, are much more willing to let go when the time arrives, and feel more confident of their teens' futures when they see them equipped with decision-making skills.

If you have not been allowing many choices for your teen, it is not too late to begin. Start with easier choices and offer more opportunities according to your teen's response. (It is helpful to use the communication techniques from chapters 6 and 7 as your relationship changes.)

■ Cautions

Do not offer a choice when no choice exists. If it is time to leave the playground, don't ask your toddler if he is ready to go. (What toddler is ever ready to leave the playground?) Offer a distracting choice instead. "In five minutes it will be time to leave. You have time for one more activity; would you like to go on the slide or on the swings?" If your struggle is over using a seatbelt in the car, don't ask your child if he wants to put his seatbelt on. Use a distracting choice instead. "Do you want to put your seatbelt on by yourself, or should I help?" or state it as a given: "It is time to put your seatbelt on before I start the car."

Don't offer a choice with a consequence you are unwilling to carry out. If it is too far to walk to school (and therefore unacceptable as a consequence of missing the bus), don't offer it as an alternative. Children are very quick to know whether or not you are willing to do what you say.

Don't offer an unlimited choice unless you are certain you are willing to discuss all alternatives as possibilities. Do you really mean "What shall we do this weekend?" Rephrase your question as a limited choice. "Shall we go to the library, go roller-skating or just lounge around this Saturday?"

Offer wider choices for older children. A toddler may choose between two pajama outfits for bed. A preschooler might choose between three school outfits for preschool. A ten-year-old can probably choose his own clothes for school each day.

■ When to use this technique

As a decision-making tool: Offer choices to your children whenever you remember to do so; whenever a reasonable choice exists that you do not have a strong opinion about. Simple choices include: a choice between two different juices in the morning, a choice between half of a sandwich or a whole sandwich, picking out the color of a new coat or choosing books at the library.

One couple described a weeklong, two-car vacation they took with their in-laws and their two-year-old child, Janey. Each morning the parents asked Janey which car she would like to ride in. The toddler could choose between mom's car and dad's car. After a few days, Janey's uncle asked her father, "Why do you keep switching the car seat back and forth between cars? Why don't you make her stay in one car to minimize the work?"

Janey's father replied, "Do you notice the excitement of that decision each morning on Janey's face? Janey has no control over the other aspects of our trip. But she can control which car she rides in, and she loves it. Did you notice how good she is on the long car rides?"

Janey's father was willing to put forth some extra energy to help his young daughter practice making decisions, gain positive self-esteem for her input, and feel that she had some personal power. Janey's excitement in this morning ritual made her feel good about herself, more interested in the trip and less prone to whining or complaining.

As a distracting choice: Use choices to distract a young child from a power struggle. Two-year-old Tony had a habit of asking for cookies as soon as his mom went near the kitchen to cook or clean. Tony's mother would refuse him, and they were off on another battle. One day Tony's mother offered him a choice between two healthy snacks, which distracted him from the cookies. Then she began letting him choose between two little kitchen "chores," such as handing her cooking items or wiping plastic dishes. Tony loved to share this time with her, and soon forgot to ask for a cookie.

With a consequence: Use a choice with a consequence when the child is more resistant to change. Four-year-old Anna and her father frequently quarreled because Anna did not like to pick up her toys. Anna's father tried distracting choices, such as, "Do you want to pick up the blocks first, or the dolls?" But Anna didn't want to pick up any toys. Anna's father offered her a choice: "You may pick up the toys and put them away for tomorrow, or I will pick up the toys and put them up for three days. You choose." When Anna did not clean up, her father put her toys up out of reach, where she would see them and not forget about them. It didn't take long for Anna to accept her new responsibilities in order to keep her toys close at hand. The problem and the quarreling disappeared.

■ Ages of children

Offer choices to children two years and older to help build decision-making skills. Distracting choices work best for toddlers and young preschoolers. Choices combined with consequences tend to change behavior quickly with children of all ages.

Teens, in particular, need to be given opportunities to practice making choices, because teens have decisions to make every day that do not include parents.

EXERCISES

Choices

Practical Exercise

What distracting choice could you use in each of the following situations:

1. Your toddler won't put on his coat to go to the store.

2. Your toddler is unwilling to leave his friend's house.

3. Your preschooler refuses to set the table.

4. Your school-age child tries to get out of doing his homework.

Choices

What choice could you use with a logical consequence in each of the following situations:

5. Your school-age child doesn't want the food you cooked for dinner.

6. Your preschooler just hit the little girl who is visiting your house.

7. Your toddler keeps climbing on your lap and pulling at your glasses as you try to talk to your visitor.

8. Your teen (who borrowed the family car) came home one hour late for curfew.

9. Your toddler screams in the grocery store if he can't have the sweets he wants.

10. Your teen expects you to make her lunch for school.

Personal Exercise

1. What is the age of your child?

2. Has she/he been making choices in the past?

3. What would be some simple choices she/he could make now?

4. Describe a discipline situation that recurs frequently (e.g., not wanting to go to bed).

5. What aspect of the situation is *not* negotiable (e.g., going to bed by 8 p.m.)?

6. What distracting choices could you use in this situation?

7. Could you use consequences as a choice in this situation? ("You may go to bed now and I will read you two stories, or you may delay and not have time for any stories.")

Natural Consequences

Two sons went camping with their fathers. On the second night, after they had pitched their tents, the fathers noticed the boys had left their boots outside the tent. The evening sky was filling with gray clouds. One father pointed out to the boys that rain at night meant wet boots in the morning, and an uncomfortable march the next day. Grumbling, the boys put their boots away.

When the first man returned to his own tent, the other father said, "I saw the boots too. But I wasn't going to say anything."

Both fathers wanted to teach their sons an important lesson about camping. One father instructed the boys, and saved them an unpleasant hike. The second father was willing to let the boys experience some discomfort so the lesson would be remembered. The second father was using a natural consequence, an excellent way to teach self-discipline.

A natural consequence is the result of a child's action that comes about naturally without parent intervention. The result may occur because of natural laws (boots left out in the rain will get wet and the next day's hike will be uncomfortable), or because of society's laws (if you drive over the speed limit you may get a speeding ticket). The noted educator Herbert Spencer originally coined the term natural consequences. However, the concept was expanded and popularized by Alfred Adler and his student and colleague, Rudolf Dreikurs.

How to use this technique

Natural consequences occur by themselves. Parents do not have to create them. Parents *do* need to monitor natural consequences to be sure they will not seriously hurt the child.

The child learns from experience. Charles goes to the job interview in sloppy clothes. He doesn't get the job. When Timothy continually skips practicing his clarinet, he is asked to drop band.

Think through a problem your child is dealing with. Ask yourself: (a) Is there a natural consequence to my child's behavior? (b) Is this consequence acceptable (not too severe)? (c) Will this consequence work (that is, will it change my child's behavior)? and (d) Am I willing to sit back, do nothing, and let my child learn from his own behavior? If the answer to all four of these questions is "yes," then natural consequences may be a good technique to try in this situation. If one or more of your answers is "no," it would be better to choose a different technique.

For parents, the hardest part of natural consequences is to refrain from intervening. We don't want our children to be hurt or disappointed. We don't want them to make the same mistakes we did. But our natural inclinations—suggestions, advice, nagging and lectures—are less than effective in changing our child's behavior. Advice and nagging do not teach internal controls very well. And constantly bailing out children—bringing the forgotten gym shoes to school or driving the teen who misses the bus—does not teach responsibility either. Many times we are actually more helpful if we sit back and say nothing. Silence is also a good way to handle the situation afterward. The child has learned the lesson from the consequence; he doesn't need "I told you so" (although sometimes a parent-child discussion is helpful).

The problem with natural consequences is that sometimes the consequences are too severe, and therefore not acceptable. We don't teach Jacob to stay out of the street by natural consequences. We don't teach Elizabeth to wear mittens by letting her fingers get frostbitten. Some parents may feel that the consequences of lower grades or broken toys are too severe. Also, some situations may not have a natural consequence. When Karen hits her baby brother, there is no naturally occurring event that teaches her hitting is wrong.

When there are no natural consequences for an undesirable behavior, or if the consequences are too severe and therefore not acceptable, parents can create their own consequences for the child (see "Logical Consequences," chapter 8).

■ Why is this technique valuable?

. Natural consequences—those that occur automatically without parent intervention—are great teachers of self-discipline. If Sammy leaves his bike out in the rain, it rusts. If Sarah doesn't do her homework, she receives a lower grade. Once a child experiences a consequence to his action, he usually adjusts his actions accordingly.

Children learn that a certain action brings a certain result. If they are unhappy with the results, they modify their actions. This allows the child the freedom and personal power of choosing behavior but places the responsibility of the child's behavior upon the child. Natural consequences save the parent from being the disciplinarian; the child learns the lesson on her own.

Natural Consequences

1. Is there a natural consequence to my child's behavior?

2. Is this consequence acceptable (not too severe)?

3. Will this consequence work (will it change my child's behavior)?

4. Am I willing to sit back, do nothing, and let my child learn from his own behavior in this situation?

   If the answer to all four of these questions is "yes," then natural consequences may be a good technique to try in this situation.

■ Cautions

Are there natural consequences to your child's specific behavior? If not, choose another technique.

Is the consequence acceptable (not too severe)? Parents will disagree on this one. Are lower grades acceptable if the child learns and grows from the experience? How about the child who leaves his toys lying around, which are stepped on and broken? Some parents say yes, the child learned his lesson and the problem no longer aggravates everyone. Other parents say no, toys are too expensive; I'd rather teach him the lesson in a different way. What if the consequence is a broken friendship, a spoiled birthday party or a stomachache? In each case, the parent must weigh the effects of the consequence against the strength of the lesson. For one child, a spoiled birthday party would be devastating. Devastating consequences shape a child's memories far into adulthood: choose a different way to help the child learn the lesson.

Will the natural consequence change your child's behavior? Each child is different. Lower grades may spur one child to get his homework done, but might not influence another child at all. If the natural consequence will not teach a child something valuable, then choose a different technique.

Are you able to sit back, do nothing, and let your child learn from his own behavior in this situation? If natural consequences exist for a situation, if they are not too serious or devastating, and if they will help your child establish inner controls, you have the potential for an excellent learning situation. Can you let go and let it happen? Then try it; it will probably work well for everyone. But if you can't let go, then don't worry about it. Choose a different technique.

■ When to use this technique

Whenever you are able to answer "yes" to the four questions listed under "Cautions."

■ Ages of children

Natural consequences are effective for children of all ages.

EXERCISES

Natural Consequences

Practical Exercise

What are the natural consequences of the following situations?

1. The child touches a hot stove.

2. The child won't eat her dinner.

3. The child stays up watching television very late on a school night.

4. The child won't share her toys.

5. The child hits his sister.

6. The child cheats on an exam at school.

7. The teen tells a friend's secret after promising she wouldn't.

8. The child throws her clothes on the floor rather than hanging them up.

9. The teen cancels a babysitting job at the last minute.

10. The teen spends her money on frivolous items.

Personal Exercise

Describe a situation with your child that you would like to modify by using natural consequences.

1. Undesirable behavior:

2. What would the natural consequences be for this behavior?

3. Is the natural consequence acceptable (not too severe)?

4. Do you think the natural consequence will change your child's behavior in this situation? Why or why not?

5. Are you able to sit back, do nothing, and let your child learn from his/her own behavior in this situation?

Chapter 6

Communication: Active Listening and "I Messages"

COMMUNICATION
- Family Meetings
- Creative Problem-Solving
- "I Messages"
- Active Listening
- Natural Consequences
- Choices

PREVENTION
- Substitution

Good things happen between parents and children when they talk about what is important to them. Communication is the basis for mutual trust and respect.

In addition, effective communication can clarify and eliminate problems before they escalate. The bigger the problem, the more important it is for the involved parties to communicate in order to resolve it.

Don't skip this chapter if your children are very young. Even babies and toddlers without language at their command are able to understand much about the world around them, often significantly more than we give them credit for. The first two communication techniques, slightly modified, are excellent methods to help young children develop language skills.

Communication techniques have many advantages when used with children, and also with other adults in our lives. These techniques are well known and respected in our world today—they are taught not only on university campuses, but also at business seminars, staff development trainings and community workshops. Effective communication is a major ingredient in a healthy family.

Four techniques comprise the communication section of the gradient: active listening, used as a tool to understand what your child really means; "I messages" to state your position without tearing down self-esteem; creative problem-solving; and family meetings.

Active Listening

Because our minds can hear and process much faster than a person speaks, it is tempting to use the extra time while listening to prepare our own responses, rather than to actively listen to what the other person says. In addition, sometimes meaning is lost between the encoding of an idea into words, the expression of the words, the hearing of the words and the decoding of the idea. The result of all this is the breakdown of communication. People often talk toward one another, but do not transfer ideas clearly.

COMMUNICATION: Encoding and Decoding an Idea

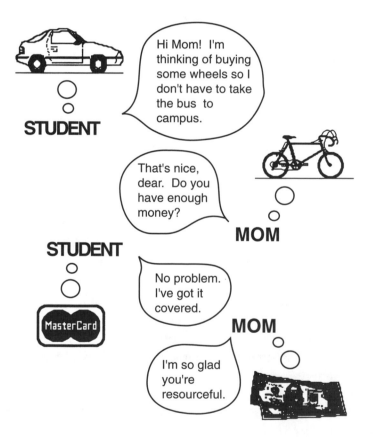

Carl Rodgers, father of person-centered counseling, coined the words "reflective listening" to name a specific way of listening during the counseling session. Rodgers felt that people could solve their own problems if they had a chance to talk them out to another person who genuinely listened to them. Reflective listening was the process of reflecting back to the client what the counselor thought he heard and understood. In other words, the counselor checked out what he heard to make sure it was what the client meant. If it was misunderstood, the client corrected the counselor. If the client felt understood, he generally confirmed his words and continued to talk. Carl Rodgers' system of counseling was acclaimed by many, and continues today to be an important counseling theory.

Active listening—very similar to reflective listening—became popular when Thomas Gordon published *P.E.T.: Parent Effectiveness Training*. Gordon describes active listening as a specific technique parents can use to encourage their children to talk about their problems. Using his own words, the parent feeds back his impression of what the child is communicating. The child confirms the feedback as accurate or corrects the misunderstanding, and continues talking. By talking out her feelings, the child finds insight into her own problem and is often able to solve it herself.

Since Rodgers and Gordon outlined their ideas, many other psychologists have used and taught reflective or active listening, sometimes calling it by other names. But the basic idea remains the same. Active listening is an effective tool a parent can use to tune in to his child's needs and ideas. Active listening builds positive parent-child relationships and encourages internal controls.

How to use this technique

The purpose of active listening is to encourage the child to talk about what is on her mind. To do this, the parent takes the child's feelings seriously and rephrases them to let her know she is genuinely understood. The parent feeds back in his own words his impression of what the child means. The child responds "yes (that's what I meant)" or "no, I meant..." and continues talking.

Three steps outline the process of active listening:
1. listen carefully to what your child is saying,
2. formulate in your mind what your child is expressing,
3. describe in your own words the feelings she has just expressed to you.

Helpful phrases to start with are *"Sounds like…"* or *"You feel…"* or *"I hear you saying…."*

Active listening example:

   Tamika (seven years old) has been talking happily to her brother at the breakfast table. But as she puts her coat on, she says in a quiet voice: "I don't want to go to school today, Mom."

   Mom: "You feel anxious about something at school."

   Tamika: "I like school, Mom. I just don't like riding the bus."

   Mom: "Sounds like something happened on the bus that you didn't like."

   Tamika: "That's right. Those two boys sitting behind me keep pulling my hair."

   Mom: "You feel upset when those boys tease you."

   Tamika: "Yes! I told the bus driver about it, and she said I could sit in a different seat. She also told the boys to stop."

   Mom: "But you're concerned they might keep teasing you."

   Tamika: "Well, yes. But I guess I could try it today, and see if they stop."

Active listening is used *instead of* rational explanations, advice or suggestions. People have a hard time listening to explanations or advice at the beginning of a discussion. However, once they feel understood, they are more willing to look at a problem objectively.

Problem-solving works best *after* the child has felt that someone has listened to her. Use enough active listening responses to allow the child to completely explain her feelings. Many times the child is able to solve her own problem; at other times, active listening might lead into problem-solving between child and parent.

The main mistake parents make during active listening is parroting, or repeating back the exact words of their child.

*Parroting, or how **not** to actively listen:*

> Tamika: "I don't want to go to school today, Mom."
> Mom: "You feel like you don't want to go to school today."
> Tamika (with a frown): "That's what I just said, Mom!"

To avoid parroting, paraphrase your child's feelings *in your own words.*

Sometimes active listening involves interpreting, or guessing the child's feelings. It's okay to guess. Guessing a highly charged emotion often opens up a difficult topic, and such discussions offer chances for deeper sharing, for intimacy. If a parent's guess is wrong, the child will correct the parent's misconception and communication can continue.

Guessing during active listening:

> Tamika: "I don't want to go to school today, Mom."
> Mom: "You're upset because I wouldn't let you wear your new dress."
> Tamika: "No, I'm not mad about that. I don't like riding the bus."

Handle irrational fears with the same feedback technique.

Active listening for irrational fears:

> Tamika: "I don't want to go to bed in the dark, Mom."
> Mom: "Sometimes it can be scary in the dark."
> Tamika: "I think about the bad witch on Sleeping Beauty. I'm afraid of her."
> Mom: "Sounds like you might be nervous that the bad witch is more than a TV character."
> Tamika: "I know, Mom. I know she's just make-believe on TV. But it still bothers me to think about it."
> Mom: "How about if we leave a night light on, and I come back to check on you a couple of times?"
> Tamika: "Sounds good. And leave the door open."

Don't forget that active listening also works very well with other adults—your spouse, your boss, irate customers, your coworkers, your father-in-law. It is an excellent way to help others feel understood (and therefore be more open to listening to your viewpoint).

Active Listening

1. Listen carefully to what your child is saying.
2. Formulate in your mind what your child is expressing.
3. Describe in your own words the feelings he has just expressed to you.
   "Sounds like..."
   "You feel..."
   "I hear you saying..."

■ Why is this technique valuable?

Active listening enhances parent-child relationships and helps resolve discipline problems. Probably the most important advantage of active listening is that it lets a child know that you understand how he feels, and gives him knowledge that his feelings are respected and valued. Giving a person your full attention says "I care about you."

Active listening keeps the lines of communication open. A person is more willing to listen to another's viewpoint after he himself feels understood.

Another important advantage of active listening is that a child will often solve his own problems if he has the chance to think about it while talking it out. What happens when you are faced with a difficult problem or decision, and you sit down with your partner or go to visit a good friend? After an hour or two of expressing feelings and exploring possibilities, you thank your friend or partner for helping you resolve the situation.

Your friend says, "Don't thank me; I didn't do anything. All I did was listen."

It's the listening that makes the difference. Talking out a complex problem helps us to sort out our feelings and to choose the most appropriate solution.

Children have similar needs to be able to talk out a problem and solve it themselves. However, parents are more likely to tell children what to do. Because we love our children, we hate to have them make the same mistakes we did. So we explain, teach, judge, offer advice or give a warning. "Have you tried..." "Why don't you..." "I told you before...." Unfortunately, these normal parental reactions do not allow a child to work out his own problem, nor do they let the child feel heard or understood.

If parents react to a child's leading statement with advice, judgment or lecturing, the child might never talk about what is really bothering him. Children (and many adults as well) often "test the waters" with a trial statement peripheral to the real problem. If the parent seems receptive, the child shares a little more, and then a little more. It takes a while for the heart of the conflict to be revealed. If we begin with trying to solve the problem instead of listening to the child, we may be addressing the wrong issue. In the example above, when Tamika stated she didn't want to go to school, her mother might have responded by explaining that children have to go to school, that learning is important, or that we all have to do things in life that we don't like. Tamika's problems on the bus might never have been discussed.

Lecturing often denies feelings:
> Karen's little brother Justin hides in Karen's bedroom and listens to her personal phone call. Upon discovering him, Karen rushes in to the kitchen, complaining loudly, "I hate my bratty little brother!"
> Mother replies, "You don't really hate him, Karen. You know you really love him."
> Karen feels victimized by her brother, misunderstood, and lectured. She leaves the kitchen, muttering under her breath.

In this example, Mother responded to the word "hate" in Karen's sentence and misunderstood what she was really trying to say. If Mother had actively listened to the feelings behind Karen's statement, the situation probably would have turned out differently.

Listening to feelings:
> After discovering that Justin listened in on a personal phone call, Karen rushes to the kitchen, complaining loudly, "I hate my bratty little brother!"
> Mother replies, "You're angry because Justin did something you didn't like."
> "Yes," says Karen. "This time he hid in my room and listened in on my phone call to Sarah!"
> "You're upset because you thought your call was private and you said things to Sarah you did not want anyone else to hear."
> "That's right! When I talk to my friends I deserve some privacy. Next time I phone Sarah, I'll check to be sure Justin is out here, and then I'll close my door."

Children often don't understand what they are feeling. They only know it feels good, or it feels bad. As parents rephrase statements during active listening, they help children name complicated feelings. Children learn what "anxious" means, or "excited," and they are able to recognize those emotions when they feel them again. They are learning a vocabulary of feelings—a basis from which to build relationships with other people as they grow up.

During the process of defining and naming emotions, children often become less afraid of their negative feelings. Active listening offers a child a safe outlet for expressing emotion. Anger or fear doesn't get bottled up inside, pushing for expression and sometimes frightening a child with its intensity.

Active listening can also be effective with very young children. My first experience of using active listening with my own toddler convinced me of the value of this technique. My first daughter was two and a half years old when my second daughter was born. Julie appeared to accept the new baby readily, with some normal jealousies and coping mechanisms. One night, as I was preparing to leave to teach a class, Julie jumped on the couch and pulled at my clothes as I tried to dress. "I should really try active listening," I told myself as I checked the clock, noting twenty minutes before I had to leave. So instead of my usual reaction (reminding her of rules and consequences), I deliberately considered what she might be feeling and launched my new technique: "You're feeling sad because Mom has to leave for class tonight."

Julie shook her head vigorously, and began to deny it. But the shake turned into a nod. Without warning, tears began to stream down her cheeks, and she erupted into great sobs. I knelt beside her and gathered her close. The next words were easy. "It's hard to be a big girl when the baby gets so much attention, and Mom is working a lot." The nods strengthened. The tears and sobs increased. "Oh my," I thought, looking at the clock. "What have I started!"

But it only took a few moments, with my big girl cradled on my lap, to suddenly find ourselves in one of our warmest discussions. We talked about how much time babies require (even if they are cute). We talked about all the neat things big girls could do—such as eating ice cream cones and swinging on the playground—that babies couldn't. We told each other how much we loved each other.

That whole wonderful conversation took only ten minutes. As I left for class that night, Julie laughed and kissed me out the door.

Active listening sometimes seems complex or stilted, but I strongly suggest that you try it. I have seen some extremely skeptical parents become its strongest advocates. *The basic idea of active listening is to put aside our own opinions and ideas, no matter what they are, and really listen to our child as he speaks.* I call it "looking through the eyes of the child"— seeing the world through his viewpoint. If the "technique" of active listening just doesn't seem natural enough, then forget the technical aspect, and just try listening to your child, giving him your total attention. The mutual joy and respect will be well worth it.

■ Cautions

There are a few cautions to using active listening, although I see each of these as positive, since they encourage our own personal growth as parents.

We must be able to accept our child's feelings, however different they are from our expectations. Sometimes as we begin an active listening session, we are not prepared to deal with the emotions that are uncovered. We must realize that, *at this moment,* this child really feels sadness, or anger, or hate or jealousy. Emotions change; they are not fixed or permanent. What a child feels right now might be dramatically different in half a day, or even half an hour. Remembering this can help us in formulating active listening responses.

Accepting a child's feelings:
Johnny (five years old): "I hate you! I hate you!"

Dad: "Right now you really feel angry with me!"

We must trust our children's capacity to work through their own feelings and to find solutions. It is often difficult to decide whether to guide our children or to let them make important decisions on their own. If parents keep in mind the goal of discipline—moving from external to internal controls—it is easier to trust that their child will be able to handle a specific problem. When he demonstrates that he can handle it, the parents' confidence in him grows, as does his own confidence in himself. He is moving closer to establishing self-control; he is growing in self-esteem. He is growing up. If we feel a bit of sadness at our children's increasing abilities (and decreasing dependence on us), it will disappear in the knowledge that we are teaching them valuable skills that will be useful for their entire lives.

There may be times when parents feel their child is not ready to work through a particular problem on his own. In this situation, combining active listening with other techniques, such as creative problem-solving (covered in chapter 7), will teach the child problem-solving skills while respecting his individuality.

■ When to use this technique

Active listening is most helpful *when the child has the problem*— when the child is speaking or acting in such a way that the parent suspects something is bothering him.

Active listening is *not* helpful *when the parent has the problem with the child.* For example, active listening is not the solution when the parent wants her son to clean his room, or her daughter to stop jumping on the furniture. When the parent has a problem with the child, the communication technique of *"I messages"* (see next section) is a good one to try.

Active listening does not work well when the parent or child is in a hurry or preoccupied with something else. If Dad just came home from work, dinner is due on the table in fifteen minutes, the baby is crying, and Tamika says she doesn't want to go to school tomorrow, it is probably not a good time for active listening. After the dishes are finished and the baby is asleep, Mom or Dad (or both) might sit down with Tamika and bring up the topic of school. If the time or desire to listen attentively is not present, then wait until it is.

Active listening is also not appropriate when children need factual information. "What's for dinner, Mom?" is probably best answered by "chicken and potatoes," and not by "you're upset because I've been working and there's not much variety for dinner" (unless, of course, that's an important issue). Constantly delving into our children's motivations for common daily interactions is not helpful. Because active listening takes thoughtful, empathic involvement, it is most useful when our children have problems or are trying to tell us something.

■ Ages of children

Active listening is ideal for preschoolers through teens (and with other adults). But it also can be adapted very effectively for preverbal toddlers, even infants. Children who grow up with active listening tend to become skillful listeners themselves.

For toddlers and babies: Remember that very young children understand much more than is apparent. We can actively listen to preverbal children by observing their behaviors, guessing at their causes of frustration or joy, and commenting on their reactions: "You're upset because I won't let you play with Mommy's book," or "You really love playing airplane with Daddy." Young children can learn to identify their feelings and realize that their feelings are respected by mom and dad. These are the seeds of positive self-esteem.

As you carry your screaming toddler off the playground, you can tell him, "It must be terribly frustrating to have to leave when you're not ready. But it's time to go home now." In this way, you reassure him that you understand how hard it is—yet the limits are still firm.

EXERCISES

Active Listening

Practical Exercise

The first step of active listening is refraining from offering advice, lecturing or suggesting. "Door openers" are statements that invite more talking and explaining from the child. "Door closers" tend to make a child feel misunderstood, defensive or resentful, or they deny a child's feelings.

Active listening takes this idea one step further by reflecting back to the child what the parent thinks the child is expressing and feeling. The chart on the following page shows examples of door openers and door closers.

Active Listening

Door Openers
Hmmm...
Oh?
Tell me more about it.
What happened?
What do you think about that?
What did she do?

Door Closers
What did you do to her?
You know the rules.
Stop whining.
It seems to me...
Why don't you...?
You don't really feel that way.

Active Listening
Sounds like...
You feel...
I hear you saying...

Child statements:

1. Six-year-old boy: "I hate my sister!"
   Door closer: "It's wrong to hate others. You don't really hate her."
   Active listening statement:

2. Eight-year-old girl: "Miss Smith is always picking on me at school."
   Door closer: "Are you goofing off in class again?"
   Active listening statement:

3. Five-year-old girl (first week of school): "Will you come to school with me today, Mom?"
   Door closer: "You're a big girl, honey. You don't need Mom."
   Active listening statement:

4. Ten-year-old girl: "I made the soccer team!"
   Door closer: "Just be sure you keep your grades up."
   Active listening statement:

5. Two-year-old boy: "Don't go to work today, Mom."
   Door closer: "I have to work to pay our bills."
   Active listening statement:

6. Seven-year-old girl: "I don't want to play with him ever again!"
   Door closer: "Oh, come on. You'll be playing with him tomorrow."
   Active listening statement:

7. Five-year-old boy: "Paul (older brother) won't play with me."
   Door closer: "He doesn't always have to play with you, you know." .
   Active listening statement:

Teen statements:
1. "I don't have anything to wear to the party. My clothes don't look right."
   Door closer: "What do you mean? Your closet is full of clothes."
   Active listening statement:

2. "All the other kids get to go to 'R' rated movies."
   Door closer: "You're not going to this one, so don't even ask."
   Active listening statement:

3. "I think Brandon's going to ask me to the senior prom."
   Door closer: "You'd better accept. You might not get another offer."
   Active listening statement:

Active Listening

4. "My science project was the worst in the class."
   Door closer: "I don't know why you are always so hard on yourself."
   Active listening statement:

5. "I never get the car when I want it."
   Door closer: "You've always got the car! I'm the one who never has it!"
   Active listening statement:

Personal Exercise

Describe a time when you felt that something was bothering your child because of his/her behavior or words:

1. When did it occur?

2. What did he/she say or do?

3. What did you say or do?

4. What was the final outcome?

5. What do you think your child was feeling at the time?

6. What active listening statement could you have used to open up communication?

7. What verbal or nonverbal signals does your child give you to show that he/she is upset?

8. How do you respond (in most cases) to these signals?

9. What active listening statement could you use to respond to these signals?

"I Messages"

Your boss tells you, "Your report was late again! Can't you do anything right? You'd better have Friday's report finished on time!" What is your reaction? Do you feel defensive? scared? resentful?

How do you feel if she phrases it like this: "I felt frustrated yesterday because I didn't have your report for the meeting. In the future, tell me if you have a problem getting a report done on time." Did the message still come through? Do you feel less defensive or resentful? Which message do you prefer?

Well-meaning parents, in their teaching, correcting and disciplining, often use "you messages," which tend to lower the child's self-esteem. "You never clean your room." "You're always fighting." "You are being irresponsible." "You messages," no matter how well-intended, convey blame. The child usually reacts defensively, trying to escape responsibility, but the message comes across regardless: "You failed again."

Besides explaining active listening, Thomas Gordon's book *Parent Effectiveness Training* also introduces "I messages" as a parenting technique. Gordon feels that by replacing the word "you" with "I," the parent's message will still be heard, but in a positive, tactful manner which allows the child to take responsibility and correct the situation. "I'm upset when siblings fight, because someone might get hurt." "I feel concerned when your homework doesn't get done, because you might get behind in your studies."

"I messages" have been used and adapted by many people since Gordon's book was first published. Just as active listening is now currently taught and used by a wide variety of people, the use of "I messages" has spread to business, teaching and many other fields. An "I message" is a tactful way to tell another person when you have a problem with that person. It explains how the first person is affected by the situation, without criticizing or blaming.

■ How to use this technique

The parent tells the child how some unacceptable behavior is making the parent feel.

There are three parts to an "I Message":

1. **When** _____
   (explain the situation)

2. **I feel** _____
   (your emotion)

3. **because** _____
   (short reason why you feel that emotion)

"I messages" do not need to be phrased in the above order, nor do they need to use the exact words suggested above. However, parents usually find this order and phrasing to be helpful, especially when first learning how to use "I messages." All three parts (situation, emotion and reason why) should be present in an "I message."

A "you message" is often interpreted by the child as a personal evaluation (usually unfavorable). An "I message" is usually interpreted as a statement by the parent requiring action.

"You message" example:
Situation: The child frequently leaves the lights on in the basement.

Common parental reaction: "When will you ever learn to turn those lights off? It costs money, you know!"

Child's feelings: "I messed up again. I'll never learn to do what I'm supposed to."

"I message" example:
Situation: The child frequently leaves the lights on in the basement.

"I Message": "When the lights are left on in the basement, I feel upset because the electric bill goes up."

Child's reaction: "Sorry, Dad. I'll go turn them off now."

The most common mistake people make when using "I messages" is to sneak in a "you message" in the second part (#2 on the previous page: "I feel..."). As children, many of us were not encouraged to express our feelings. As adults, we often still have a hard time saying how we feel. When we practice "I messages," somehow the *emotion* of the second part is translated into "I feel you should..." or "I feel you aren't ...." For example: "When the lights are left on in the basement, I feel you are being irresponsible because you're wasting electricity."

The way to avoid this common mistake is to be sure to put an *emotion* in the blank after "I feel..." Check yourself by substituting the words "I think" for the words "I feel." If "I think" makes sense in your sentence, go back and try again. ("I think you are being irresponsible...") How do you, as a parent and as a person, *feel* when the situation occurs? Tell your child.

Hidden "you message":
"When you don't do your chores on time, I feel you're shirking your duties, because the rest of us have to do your share."

In the above sentence, substituting "think" for "feel" makes sense ("I think you're shirking your duties..."), so this message does not explain the speaker's *feelings*. Instead, it sneaks in a "you message," which is less tactful and is discouraging to a child's self-esteem. "You messages" are also more likely to make a child feel defensive or rebellious. Try replacing "I feel you're shirking your duties" with an emotion, as in "I feel upset" or "I feel resentful." Telling the child how you feel encourages the child to see the situation from another viewpoint.

Parents sometimes ask me if the word "you" should be avoided completely within an "I message." Phrasing messages in a general way *does* encourage the child's self-esteem and minimize defensiveness. Try "When the lights are left on..." rather than "When *you* leave the lights on…" or "When children fight on the playground…" rather than "When *you* fight on the playground…." However, I don't think a parent needs to worry if he finds an occasional "you" slipping into the *"when"* and *"because"* parts of an "I message." The *"because"* part is particularly likely to contain acceptable uses of "you": "because I'm worried you'll get hurt" or "because I'd like you to learn how to get along with others."

But keep the "you" out of the *"I feel"* part of the "I message."

You will be surprised at your child's reaction to an "I message." In many cases, the child will respond to the need and take care of the problem. In more complex situations, the child often responds with her own feelings, and parent and child exchange thoughts and feelings about the problem. At this time, active listening (see previous section) and creative problem-solving (see next section) can be very helpful.

> *Complex "I message" example:*
>
> (single) Mother *("I message")*: "When I invite a man to dinner, I feel hurt and embarrassed when you won't say a word to him all evening."
>
> (teen) Melissa: "But Mom, I don't understand how you can invite those creeps when Dad is so much nicer."
>
> Mother *(active listening)*: "You feel I'm being disloyal to your father by seeing other men?"
>
> Melissa: "Well, yes. I can't understand why you and Dad are getting a divorce."
>
> Mother: "I hear you saying you're upset because Dad left. You wish we could have worked things out."
>
> Melissa (hugs mother): "I know we talked about it. I think I understand. But it really bothers me to see a strange man sitting in Dad's place at dinner."
>
> Mother *(problem-solving)*: "Maybe Ted wouldn't have to sit in Dad's place. Or maybe we could go out to eat."
>
> Melissa: "Maybe we could just take our plates and sit around in the living room."

■ Why is this technique valuable?

"I messages" are less threatening to a child's self-esteem than "you messages," which often judge, blame, criticize or command. A child is less likely to react defensively, to internalize negative feelings about himself, or to resist or rebel. "You forgot your lunch bucket at school again," might stimulate a child to:

- feel defensive: "It's not my fault. How am I supposed to remember it every day?"
- to feel less kind toward himself: "I'm always forgetting things. One more thing I can't do right."
- to resist or rebel: "I don't see why I have to carry that old bucket anyway. Why can't I buy lunch like the other kids do?"

An "I message" ("When you forget your lunch bucket at school, I feel frustrated because it's hard to find something to put your lunch in for the next day") explains the parent's viewpoint without blaming. It gives the child an opportunity to change his behavior on his own. "I messages" tell a child that the parent trusts him to handle the situation with respect to the parent's needs.

My first experience with using "I messages" with my children was a simple one. Fuming with displeasure, I hung up the telephone after struggling to hear a long-distance call above my daughter's loud play. I tried to swallow my anger and told her strongly, "When children play too loudly while I'm on the telephone, I'm very frustrated because I can't hear the person on the other end!"

Instead of our usual confrontation, lecture and hurt feelings, my four-year-old daughter calmly and helpfully offered, "I'm sorry, Mom. I won't do it again." Of course, at my daughter's age, the problem was not permanently solved, but the statement had defused my own anger and pointed out my need, which my daughter responded to. Instead of receiving a lecture on how she failed again—a lecture which would have reinforced a poor self-image—she took a step toward responsibility.

"I messages" help a child grow from egocentricity (viewing the world from only his own viewpoint) to a greater understanding and acceptance of other people's needs. A child is less likely to grow in these ways if he is focused on his own hurt or resistance.

"I messages" also teach a vocabulary of feelings. A child becomes more aware of different types of feelings when he hears others express them. And he is more likely to send similar messages when he encounters a problem.

I remember the time when my daughter Julie futilely tried to convince her stubborn younger sister to return her doll. "I'm angry at you!" and "I won't play with you!" were her opening lines. Jamie sat unmoved. Suddenly the expression on Julie's face changed. She sat down next to her sister and said simply, "I'm really sad when you take my special doll." Immediately Jamie's own expression softened, and she handed over the doll.

The openness of "I messages" encourages positive communication and positive relationships.

■ Cautions

Don't hide a "you message" after "I feel . . ." (see "How to use this technique," above).

Don't send only negative "I messages." "I messages" are also a great way to express your positive feelings. "When you remember to turn the lights off in the basement, I feel relieved and thankful because I don't have to go down to do it." "I feel so proud and happy that you were chosen for the lead in the school play! I know how hard you practiced."

Don't express strong feelings too mildly. "I don't like it when you hit the baby." Say what you feel in an appropriate manner. "I'm *very upset* when you hit the baby, because I'm afraid she'll be hurt!"

Be cautious when using anger in an "I message." On one hand, an "I message" can be a constructive way to vent anger, rather than hurting someone physically. But anger is a secondary emotion. That is, we feel other *primary* feelings before we feel anger. It is more effective to express these primary feelings—such as fear, resentment or frustration—in "I" statements. Anger often communicates judgment and blame. See chapter 11 for more discussion of anger.

A child may respond to an "I message" with an "I message" (or less-pleasing "you message") of her own. She may have a logical reason or complaint. Usually the best response when this happens is to *try active listening.* Find out what is bothering your child about this problem, then try more "I messages," using active listening as needed. (See the complex "I message" example on page 112.)

If your child does not respond to an "I message," you may need to state it again, perhaps more strongly. If your child still doesn't respond favorably, and you have tried active listening, I suggest combining the "I message" with another technique on the gradient, such as creative problem-solving or logical consequences. The parent's "I message" respects the child's self-esteem, but the request is backed up by a stronger technique designed to change behavior.

As with active listening, occasionally a parent feels that "I messages" are too complex or stilted to use effectively. Again, I encourage you to give them a try anyway. If it is too difficult to remember all three parts of the statement, concentrate on substituting "I" for "you." That one simple change will soften accusations and protect self-esteem. (Instead of the natural impulse to start with "you"—"You're always messing up my house!"—swallow the "you" and start with "I." "I need to have a clean house after a hard day.")

Many of us parents were not encouraged to define or share our feelings when we were children, and it may feel uncomfortable to label our feelings in an "I message." Sharing our feelings with our children encourages intimacy, the free expression of who we are. It strengthens communication and relationships with our children.

But even if we feel too uncomfortable to share our direct feelings in an "I message," we can refrain from using the accusatory "you," and we can define a situation without blaming. "The lights in the basement need to be turned off" (instead of "You left the lights on again") or "The floor needs vacuuming" (instead of "You're always skipping your chores. How lazy can you get!"). This simple shift in speech can change a child's negative reactions into a positive approach to responsibility.

▨ When to use this technique

"I messages" are most helpful when the parent has a problem concerning the child and needs a way to express it. "I messages" are also very effective when combined with other techniques on the gradient.

"I messages" can be thought out in advance for a problem situation which occurs frequently. Then, when the situation arises again, the parent is ready. Lisa had a habit of leaving her father's gardening tools lying around carelessly. Her father nagged and scolded and threatened. After learning about "I messages," Lisa's father composed and practiced this message: "When my gardening tools are left scattered around the yard, I feel upset and concerned that they'll be lost or ruined." The next time Lisa forgot to put away the tools, her father was ready with his response. Lisa was surprised not to receive his usual scolding, and the following day she remembered to put the tools away.

"I messages" can also be written down, pinned to pillows or taped to mirrors. Saying something in writing is sometimes easier than saying it verbally. One parent with five teens in her home occasionally left tactful "I message" notes on a teen's pillow. The mother also received written responses from her children on her own pillow. Sometimes the whole situation was resolved without needing to speak about it.

Remember to use positive "I" statements to encourage appropriate behaviors and to express compliments and pleasure. This is especially true if you notice your child doing something she has previously had a hard time with. "How happy I feel when I see my two children playing together and having fun!" or "I really like it when you help me fold the laundry, because it makes my job so much easier."

■ Ages of children

"I messages" work very well for any child (or adult) who is able to understand language. "I messages" for toddlers and preschoolers can be very simple: "It hurts when you hit!" or "I like it when you are gentle with the kitty."

Physically guiding young children is also a form of "I" statement. Lifting a child down from the cupboard with a serious frown and shake of your head tells her you are concerned for her safety. I encourage parents of young, preverbal children to say simple "I messages" anyway, even if they are not sure their children will understand their words. Children of any age are very good at reading nonverbal cues, such as facial expressions, gestures and tone of voice.

"I Messages"

1. When_____ (explain the situation)
2. I feel_____ (your emotion)
3. because_____ (short reason why you feel that way)

EXERCISES

Sending "I Messages"

Practical Exercise

1. Sandy, 9, keeps forgetting to bring her gym shoes to school.
   "You message": "I've told you every day this week to take your shoes to school. Why can't you remember?"
   "I message":

2. Sarah, 15, has been talking on the phone for over an hour.
   "You message": "You're tying up the phone again. You're so inconsiderate."
   "I message":

3. Robert, 5, and Jenny, 7, are playing so loudly with a new game that it is interfering with the conversation of parents in the next room.
   "You message": "Why can't you show some respect for others?"
   "I message":

4. Debbie, 10, promised to clean the cat box before the company came that evening. The job never got done.
   "You message": "You do everything you want to do, but you never do anything for me."
   "I message":

5. Peter, 17, arrived home at 1 a.m. rather than midnight, as agreed upon earlier.
   "You message": "Where have you been! You're an hour late!"
   "I message":

6. Brandon, 3, is climbing on the furniture.
    "You message": "How many times have I told you not to climb on the couch!"
    "I message":

7. Laura, 6, picked up her clothes before going out to play.
    "You message": "You're usually so messy, Laura. I'm surprised you remembered to pick up your clothes."
    "I message":

8. George, 2 years, is pulling his mother's skirt while she is trying to get dinner on the table.
    "You message": "Quit bothering me!"
    "I message":

9. Candy, age 4, is teasing the cat.
    "You message": "Don't you know any better?"
    "I message":

10. Patrick, age 11, has been watching television in the evenings instead of doing his homework.
    "You message": "You'd better shape up and turn off the TV before you get into trouble at school."
    "I message":

11. Maria, age 8, finished her dishwashing chores while in a hurry to go out to play. Some of the plates are not fully clean.
    "You message": "Why can't you take your time and do it right like your sister does?"
    "I message":

Personal Exercise

1. Describe a frequent problem with your child.
   When does it usually happen?

   What does your child do/not do?

   What is your response?

   How do you feel afterward?

   How do you think your child feels?

2. Is this a common developmental problem for your child's age?

3. Write out a sample "I message" that you could use the next time this situation occurs.
   When...

   I feel...

   because...

4. What do you think your child will say (or do) in response?

5. If your child complains about the situation, what active listening statement could you use?
   You feel...

   Sounds like...

   I hear you saying...

Chapter 7

Communication: Creative Problem-Solving and Family Meetings

Creative Problem-Solving

Creative problem-solving, a technique used widely in the business field, is when two or more people brainstorm ideas to resolve a problem. It has two important goals: to draw on a variety of ideas from people working together and to enlist the support of those people by including them in the decision-making process.

Parents and children use creative problem-solving when they explore a problem together, generate possible solutions and pick one that everyone is willing to try. Creative problem-solving can be used by one parent and one child, by a whole family, or by a teacher and a classroom of children. Adults can encourage children to use the process among themselves.

An excellent example of problem-solving in families is Thomas Gordon's "no-lose" method of solving parent-child conflicts, described in *Parent Effectiveness Training*. Gordon calls it "no-lose" because neither parent nor child "wins" at the expense of the other. Another good example is Fitzhugh Dodson's "mutual problem solving," as explained in his book *How to Discipline With Love*.

■ How to use this technique

There are five steps in creative problem-solving:

1. Define the problem and agree to try to find a solution.
2. Brainstorm ideas.
3. Eliminate inappropriate ideas.
4. Choose (by consensus) one idea to try.
5. Reevaluate after sufficient time has passed.

1. Define the problem and agree to find a solution. When two or more people are in conflict, they may perceive the problem in different ways. Dad may view the problem like this: his ten-year-old daughter Jenny is watching television more than she does her homework, and her grades are falling. Mom may view the same problem as Jenny's lack of friends and her shaky self-esteem. Jenny's view is that school is boring, she doesn't like her teacher, and television is what she enjoys most.

Identifying and clarifying the problem—sometimes several aspects of it—will assure that everyone is focused on the same topic. After talking about the problems from different viewpoints, Jenny and her parents agree to concentrate on Jenny's falling grades.

All parties in the problem-solving situation must be committed to working together to find a solution. If Dad has a hidden agenda (he wants to restrict television to weekends) and is merely going through the motions, this technique will not be effective. If a child doesn't want to participate but sits sullenly through the process, this is not the technique to use.

2. Brainstorming ideas means writing down all the ideas that come to mind, without stopping to analyze them. The developer of brainstorming in the business world, Alex Osborn, suggested four ground rules to help people come up with new ideas without feeling inhibited:

- Restrict criticism until later. Don't discuss ideas until after the brainstorming part is over. When someone starts analyzing, ideas stop flowing and people begin to concentrate on what *doesn't* work. If the rule says analyzing must wait, people feel free to mention ideas without holding back because of fear that someone would disapprove.
- Welcome wild ideas. Creative ideas are often unusual, imaginative problem-solvers. The wild idea itself may be impractical, but such ideas frequently spark related ideas in those who are listening. Also, people are less likely to feel left out or put down in a noncritical atmosphere where all ideas are acceptable.

- Ask for as many ideas as possible. The greater the number of ideas, the greater the chance of finding useful solutions.
- Seek combining and improving of ideas. Many times the best solution comes from a combination of ideas, or from changing an impractical idea to make it more effective. Write down the ideas generated during brainstorming so they can be easily discussed and not accidentally forgotten.

In the above example, Jenny and her parents generated the following list of ideas:
- Restrict television to weekends.
- Do homework before watching television at night.
- Don't worry about grades and take what you get.
- Change classrooms so the teacher doesn't bother Jenny so much.
- Invite a friend over to study several nights a week.
- Have Mom or Dad talk with Jenny's teacher.
- Have Jenny talk to her school counselor about her teacher.
- Find a tutor.
- Restrict extracurricular activities until Jenny's grades improve.
- Let Jenny go to summer camp if she can bring her grades to Bs.
- Let Jenny watch television as much as she likes if her grades are Bs or better.

3. Eliminate inappropriate ideas. After a list is generated, each idea is considered separately. Inappropriate ideas—including ideas any person is unwilling to try—are crossed off. If the list disappears, it is necessary to move back a step and brainstorm more ideas. Occasionally it might be helpful to go all the way back to the beginning to be sure that the correct problem has been addressed.

In the above example, Jenny did not want to restrict television or extracurricular activities. Jenny's parents were not willing to have Jenny change classrooms mid-semester, nor were they willing to give up hoping for improvement. Jenny did not want to talk to the counselor at this time, but she was interested in a tutor. Mom and Dad felt they could not afford a tutor.

4. Choose (by consensus) one idea to try. Consensus is different from majority rule. Majority rule means taking a vote. The trouble with using the majority's decision is that one person may wind up in the minority time after time. Also, those in the minority have a tendency to sabotage the group effort.

Consensus means everyone is willing to give the idea a try, even though they may not be in love with it. Because all members are included in the process, they are more likely to work toward results.

Jenny and her parents decided together that Jenny could have friends over to study with, and also agreed that she could attend summer camp if her grades improved to Bs or higher.

5. Reevaluate after sufficient time has passed. The problem-solving process does not always generate the best idea first. It may take several trials before the most appropriate solution is found. (But each stage is often a valuable learning process.) Evaluate the chosen idea one or two weeks later to see if it is indeed workable. If not, perhaps it can be changed slightly to produce greater satisfaction, or it may be time to go back to brainstorming again or to redefine the problem.

The first part of Jenny's solution worked well—having friends over to study increased Jenny's self-confidence, social skills and desire to succeed in school. However, despite steady progress, it became apparent that Jenny would not be able to reach a B in French that semester. Jenny's parents agreed that Jenny could still attend camp if she received a C in French and Bs or above in her other classes. In fact, Jenny did attend camp, and she continued to maintain or improve her grades the following semester. In addition, without much attention, Jenny's hours of watching television decreased.

Adults can modify this technique to encourage children to problem-solve among themselves (see "When to use this technique").

■ Why is this technique valuable?

Creative problem-solving develops creative thinking skills in children. It also teaches social skills, such as learning how to negotiate and handle relationships. These skills will be useful in our children's careers and personal lives for as long as they live.

Because our society is shifting more and more to a cooperative one, cooperative problem-solving skills will become more and more desirable and necessary for successful social and business interactions. The business world has discovered that increasing worker input into the organization increases profits by encouraging and stimulating new ideas and by increasing worker satisfaction. Employees are much more likely to try to resolve issues and to try out ideas if they are allowed to be part of the decision-making process.

The same two advantages in business are present in families: (a) more ideas are generated from people working together, and (b) children are more willing to follow through on decisions because they have been involved in the process. One person's idea may spark additions or changes from another person. Both sides become more willing to consider another's viewpoint.

Problem-solving techniques resolve discipline problems without angry confrontation. Parenting problems can easily dissolve into a struggle for power. Whenever one side wins, the other side must lose. Whether the parent loses or the child loses, the situation has caused hurt, anger or resentment. This is a win/lose situation.

Creative problem-solving is a win/win situation. Because both sides are involved in the process, both sides are more willing to try the solution. Having input throughout the process assures the child that her feelings will be considered as well. Because of her investment in the solution, she is less likely to sabotage the effort.

■ Cautions

The first few times creative problem-solving is used, *it may take some revising and refining to mutually agree upon a realistic solution.* However, as creative problem-solving is used more and more, children and parents will become more adept at finding helpful solutions with a shorter processing time. This technique may require a longer time to implement than other discipline techniques, but in the long run, time and energy will be saved as children learn how to solve problems without parental intervention.

Be sure to define the conflict clearly. Be specific. Use phrases such as "throws school clothes on floor" rather than "is sloppy."

Don't turn down any suggestions during the brainstorming. Let everyone participate.

Don't compromise on consensus. If you cannot come up with one idea that everyone is willing to try, go back and brainstorm more ideas. In large groups, ask those in the minority how the idea could be changed to make it acceptable. If after much discussion the group is still divided, discuss whether ideas could be alternated or combined.

Be sure to evaluate. Sometimes, after a problem-solving decision has been implemented, people realize that a different issue is actually causing the problem. In this case, it is helpful to go back to the beginning, redefine the problem and begin again.

Creative problem-solving takes more effort than imposing an adult decision upon a child, but it solves problems more effectively. The final result may be what the parent had privately chosen and would have imposed without discussion. But the process of discovering and choosing that solution together will make implementing that decision much easier and with greater probability of success.

When to use this technique

Creative problem-solving can be used whenever there is conflict: between parent and child, between child and child, and between groups of children and one or more adults.

Adults can help children problem-solve by acting as a facilitator. This is particularly helpful:

1. *When a child runs to tell tales,* ask him, "What are you going to do about that?" If the child doesn't know, ask him, "What are some things you could try?" If the child still isn't sure, give him a suggestion or two, and encourage him to try it. In this way, the child is discouraged from the payoff of tattle-telling (getting the other child in trouble). He is encouraged to try to solve the problem himself. If one solution doesn't work and the child comes running back to the adult, help the child choose another suggestion. Problem-solving is not always instantaneous; it often takes more than one try. (About tattle-telling: teach children when it is important to tell; e.g., if someone is hurt.)

2. *During sibling (or other) fights,* ask the children to define the problem and to come up with possible solutions. From this point, older children can usually continue their own problem-solving, focusing on the solution rather than the problem. Younger children often have to be helped the rest of the way—choosing a compromise they both agree to, implementing the decision and checking to make sure it works.

Example with young children:
Two-year-old Kevin grabbed the truck away from his four-year-old sister Maggie. Maggie grabbed it back; Kevin hit her.

Mother knelt between them and asked them, "Should I take the toy away or can you work it out?"

"We can work it out," said Maggie. Kevin nodded.

"What can you do so you will both be happy?" asked Mother. Neither child had an answer. Both wanted the truck. Mother said, "How about if we set the timer for 5 minutes and take turns?"

Both children agreed. Kevin was insistent that he have the first turn, but Maggie didn't mind if she was second. Mother set the clock and Kevin gave up the truck readily when the bell sounded.

Example with school-age children:

Moira, age 8, and Holly, age 9, were fighting over a game they were playing. "Can you work it out yourselves, or do you have to go into separate rooms for awhile?" asked Dad.

The girls assured him they could work it out themselves, but they didn't know how to go about it.

"Can you take turns?" suggested Dad.

"Moira had first turn last time," said Holly, "and she won't let me go first this time."

"But Holly won right away, and we didn't get to play hardly at all," complained Moira.

"Hey," said Holly. "Let's play the new game I got for my birthday."

The quarrel was over.

Example with preteens:

Jessica, age 12, is visiting her friend Selena, age 11, on a rainy afternoon. They cannot decide what to do. Jessica wants to watch television, but Selena does not. "Why don't you sit down and make a list," suggests Selena's mother. The girls generate a long list, including a few items that are not possible in the rain (biking), some that are not acceptable to Selena's mother (hanging out at the mall), and some that are silly (redecorating the house). After crossing out the unacceptable items, the girls finish with a list of four activities they plan to do during the afternoon: baking cookies, trying out new hairstyles, reading and craft-making.

■ Ages of children

Creative problem-solving works particularly well with school-age children and teens. As children grow older, parental control loses its power. Through creative problem-solving, children learn problem-solving skills and have appropriate situations to express their own personal power.

Preschoolers and older toddlers need help from adults to use this technique. However, this is a great age at which to introduce the idea of creative problem-solving. Learning these skills at an early age will help resolve conflicts and set the stage for cooperative interactions as children grow older. Use simple variations of creative problem-solving with younger children. Teach problem-solving techniques by encouraging children to help you solve a simple problem. "What should we do about breakfast? We're out of milk." (Have toast instead of cereal. Run down to the store to buy some milk. Borrow some milk from the neighbor.)

Creative problem-solving does not work well with babies and young toddlers, since they are too young to understand the concepts.

Creative Problem-Solving

1. Define the problem and agree to try to find a solution.
2. Brainstorm ideas.
3. Eliminate inappropriate ideas.
4. Choose (by consensus) one idea to try.
5. Reevaluate after sufficient time has passed.

EXERCISES

Creative Problem-Solving

Practical Exercise

What's wrong with the following creative problem-solving situations? How could they be improved?

1. Mom and Dad sat down with their two sons—John, age 6, and Zach, age 11—to choose a place for their summer vacation. After brainstorming a list, they voted on the remaining places. Mom said she liked camping. Zach and John voted to visit the capitol, but Dad said they had to go camping because it cost less.

2. The family gathered together to work out the problem of caring for their dog—everyone seemed too busy to walk him. "My friend James can walk him," offered four-year-old Bobby during brainstorming. Dad ignored him and concentrated on writing down the serious suggestions. Eventually the family decided to take turns walking the dog. Bobby kept forgetting when it was his turn to walk the dog, so on Tuesdays the dog did not get a walk.

3. "You're not serious enough, Joe," said Mother. "What can we do to solve that?" Mother and Joe, age 8, brainstormed ideas about decreasing Joe's silliness. They couldn't come up with any solutions that both could agree on.

Personal Exercise

1. Describe an issue that you and your child(ren) never seem to resolve adequately.

2. Are you willing to try to resolve this issue through creative problem-solving? Do you think your child is willing? (If your child is not willing, choose a different problem that your child *would* be willing to try to resolve in this way.)

3. Define the problem simply and clearly according to your viewpoint.

4. How do you think your child would define the problem?

5. Brainstorm possible solutions to this problem. Let your creativity loose.

6. What possible solutions to this problem do you think your child would suggest?

7. What possible solutions on the total combined list would you eliminate? Which ones do you think your child would eliminate?

8. Which solutions do you think you and your child could both agree on?

9. Now try this exercise with your child. Did it work out the way you thought it would? How was it different from your "practice" questions above?

10. Are both you and your child willing to try the solution you chose?

11. When will you begin?

12. When will you reevaluate?

The Family Meeting

"Rita keeps going into my room and taking my pencils and paper without asking," said Angelo.

"Someone keeps going into my study and using my computer without permission," said Dad, with a meaningful look at Angelo.

"Why don't you bring it up at the family meeting?" asked Mom.

The family meeting (also called family council) occurs when family members meet together on a regular basis to express their ideas and make choices as a group.

The idea of the family meeting originated with Alfred Adler and his student and colleague, Rudolf Dreikurs. Good descriptions of family meetings in action are found in Dreikurs' *Children: The Challenge*, in Loren Grey's *Discipline Without Fear*, and in Painter and Corsini's *The Practical Parent*.

■ How to use this technique

For a family meeting to be successful, it must fit the needs of a particular family. Each individual family decides how meetings are organized and what rules to follow. The following four guidelines are suggested for all families:

1. The family meets together on a regular basis.
2. Meeting rules are decided on by the family.
3. Anything can be discussed, positive as well as negative.
4. Decisions are made by consensus.

1. The family meets together on a regular basis. Everyone in the family is a member. Meetings could occur weekly, or they might occur once or twice per month. Some families prefer weeknights, finding that weekends tend to be too busy. Other families say that Sunday afternoons or evenings are best. Whatever time the family chooses, it should not be changed without everyone's approval. Holding a family meeting during one person's usual night out causes hurt feelings and less commitment to attending future meetings. The Rodrigues family, in the example at the beginning of this section, meet weekly on Sunday afternoons at 4 p.m.

Many families plan a fun activity to follow after a family meeting. This encourages all family members to participate, to look forward to meetings, and to keep meetings short. Fun activities depend on family interests—playing a board game together, going for a walk or having ice cream are some suggestions. The Rodrigues family enjoys "Build Your Own Sundae" after family meetings, choosing from a whole array of ice cream flavors and toppings. There is very little trouble getting people to participate.

2. *Meeting rules are decided on by the family.* Some families like to keep rules few and simple, others choose more order and organization. Family members should decide what works best for them. Rotating the chairperson ensures that all members have a chance to control the discussion. In addition, it allows children the experience of trying to keep order and of trying to ensure that all opinions are heard. Some families choose a secretary—a person who keeps track of what was decided and who reads the minutes in the next meeting.

Each family decides whether all family members are required to attend meetings. It often works just as well not to have such a requirement—people who miss meetings find that decisions have been made without their input. They may also find their names beside the least popular chore on the chore list for the week.

The Rodrigues family has chosen the following meeting rules:
- The chairperson position rotates each meeting.
- Concerns should be expressed positively, so that no one is hurt.
- Agenda issues are not talked about outside of meetings.
- Items are discussed in order, per agenda.
- Each meeting should end on a positive note.
- Meetings may not exceed one hour.

3. *Anything can be discussed, positive as well as negative.* Any subject that is a matter of family concern can be brought up and discussed. This is an excellent place to use creative problem-solving (discussed earlier in this chapter). The steps of creative problem-solving allow all persons to contribute ideas and encourage all persons to work together to select a solution.

To keep the meeting from becoming a gripe session, include discussions of positive activities. Use the opportunity to congratulate a person on a job well done—whether the work was at school, on the job or at home. Plan family activities together; discuss vacations.

Each week, the Rodrigues family tapes an agenda on the refrigerator with major topics for discussion at the next family meeting. The agenda includes a few blank spaces for people to pencil in specific concerns that surface during the week. The family keeps faithfully to the agenda during the meeting, assuring that the meeting will not run overtime because new items arise. The last item on each agenda is recognition of any accomplishments by family members that week. This positive ending is always enjoyed by everyone.

4. *Decisions are made by consensus.* Although some families use majority vote, making decisions by consensus has several advantages. With consensus—when everyone agrees to give it a try—no one is in the minority. All persons have a direct say in the solution and thus are more willing to make the decision work. Because coming to a mutual agreement is more difficult than taking a vote, all members must work harder at cooperating, compromising and taking turns. These are excellent skills for children to learn and practice.

At their family meeting that Sunday, the Rodrigues family talked about using items that belonged to other family members. They used the process of creative problem-solving to come up with these rules:

- the borrower must ask permission first,
- the borrowed items must be returned (or the study cleaned up) within a reasonable length of time,
- if supplies are used up, they must be replaced,
- if any of these rules are broken, the lender has the right to refuse loaning for two weeks.

Mother thought all the rules were reasonable. Dad thought the penalty should be four weeks. Rita did not like the idea of replacing the paper she borrowed. Angelo thought the penalty should be one week. But all of the Rodrigues family members agreed to give the rules a try as they were stated, and to evaluate after one month to see how it was working.

■ Why is this technique valuable?

Family meetings promote communication, cooperation and problem-solving skills. Within the safety of the family environment, people are encouraged to practice skills that will be useful throughout their lives. Taking turns, listening to others, facilitating discussion, generating ideas and learning to compromise are a few examples of skills developed during family meetings.

Family meetings offer time to consider solutions to common problems. Families usually realize that various conflicts exist within the household, but are often too busy to sit down and figure out what to do about them. We tend to deal with conflict when we are right in the middle of it. However, the best time to consider a problem is when tempers are cool and objectivity is high.

Family meetings allow all family members a say in matters that concern the whole family. Choices made by consensus are usually carried out by willing people, since all have had a say in the decision. The result is less grumbling and greater cooperation.

Don't give up on this technique before you have given it a try. Family meetings are not as complex as they sound. They do not require any special personality or expertise. The short time spent together saves time during the week—time formerly spent in frustration, conflict or ineffective decision-making.

■ Cautions

The first solutions may not be the best solutions. Families often need time to adjust to group problem-solving. The Rodrigues family decided to rotate chores weekly. But after two weeks, they realized that each family member preferred specific chores and didn't want to keep changing. In the Woods family meeting, it was decided to let the person who finished dinner last be the one to do the dishes. Less than a week had passed before they realized how unpleasant it was gulping down dinner! Problem-solving gave each family the understanding of how to negotiate a course of action. Practical experience helped them discard one decision and choose another more appropriate to their needs.

Discuss positive activities as well as negative situations. Emphasis on the positive keeps feelings high and people interested. Too much griping, especially if not resolved, will cancel interest and attention. Also, if one or more people dominate meetings, the other members will soon decide that meetings are not in their favor or worth their commitment. Lynn and Janet Morley, two teenagers, tended to use up family meeting time complaining about phone privileges and getting stuck with each other's chores. After a few meetings, the two younger children became bored and refused to attend. The Morley parents decided to use creative problem-solving with Lynn and Janet outside the meetings. They introduced positive topics during family meeting time, such as planning a roller-skating party and a fishing trip. At the end of the next meeting, the Morleys went out for a family pizza. The result of this new focus was immediate—the younger children began to participate again, while the two older sisters became aware of other, broader issues and began to fight less on their own.

Make sure everyone is able to participate. If one child is consistently quiet, sullen or shy, try directing questions to him first before asking the other members. Eight-year-old Jimmy Bower spoke very little during the Bower family meetings. He didn't seem to have opinions and tended to agree with anything proposed by his parents or older siblings. Dad (when he became chairperson) asked Jimmy how he felt about the new shared-room arrangements they had tried that past week.

Jimmy shrugged. "It's okay, I guess."

Dad persisted. He asked specific questions. "What do you like about sharing a room with Ben?"

Jimmy was silent for a moment. Dad waited.

"I like the bigger closet and more room to put my stuff."

"Is there anything you don't like?"

"Well, Ben always wakes me up when he comes home late. And when he studies after I go to bed, the light keeps me awake."

Ben agreed to try to be more quiet if he came in late. Dad offered to let Ben use his den to study at night, if Ben asked in advance. The family had been unaware of Jimmy's feelings, but pitched in quickly to help solve his concerns. Jimmy was surprised at the result of his statements, and a little pleased with himself. With coaching from Dad, the other family members (especially when they were acting as chairperson) continued to draw out Jimmy's ideas. Jimmy's self-confidence grew, and the family felt more comfortable when he was no longer overlooked at meetings.

Keep meetings to a reasonable length. As meetings run longer, patience runs shorter. If meetings consistently run overtime, members will no longer want to come. One hour is probably the maximum length of an effective family meeting. Families with young children may find that 15 minutes is sufficient.

▇ When to use this technique

Try using family meetings if you have children who are three years or older. Choose a day and time that is convenient to all members of your family. Meet on a regular basis, if possible. Spend time in the first meeting describing how a family meeting works and selecting a few rules to begin with.

If you have one or more family members who are not interested in attending the family meeting, try holding meetings anyway. The person who boycotts the meetings may become interested later when he realizes his opinions and wishes are not being considered in family decisions.

Family Meeting

1. The family meets together on a regular basis.
2. Meeting rules are decided upon by the family.
3. Anything can be discussed—positive as well as negative.
4. Decisions are made by consensus.

■ Ages of children

School-age and teenage children respond particularly well to the increased involvement of family meetings. These older ages enjoy giving input, discussing and resolving situations. They also like the challenge of leading meetings and tend to emerge with a greater appreciation of the difficulties of leadership.

Preschool children can understand the idea of working things out in family meetings. They can contribute opinions and can help generate solutions. The preschool years are a good time to introduce the concepts of cooperation and communication as a family unit, since preschoolers are interested in belonging and social interaction.

Toddlers rarely operate effectively in family meetings. However, toddlers can attend family meetings with older children and begin to learn the process of cooperation through modeling. Family meetings work very well with a group of children of various ages.

EXERCISES

Family Meetings

Practical Exercise

What could improve the effectiveness of these family meeting situations?

1. The Jones family began holding family meetings twice a month. They decided to use Robert's Rules of Order to familiarize their children with proper meeting etiquette. The family meetings brought up some sensitive topics, but the children seemed reluctant to talk freely. "I get confused knowing when I can talk," said six-year old Amy. "It's too stilted," said fifteen-year-old Mark. The Jones family found it hard to reach a consensus when problem-solving.

2. The Green family began meeting informally once per month. Many small problems were resolved and a number of fun outings were planned by majority rule. Everyone in the family thought the meetings were great except Amanda, age 9. Amanda was quiet and tended not to express her feelings. She had voted with the minority in the last eight voting issues. Lately she had started skipping meetings.

3. Chuck, age 16, complained, "I was going to the movies on Friday night. Now I have to cancel for a crummy family meeting."

    "You won't miss much if you skip it," said George, age 13. "All we do is complain about chores, and Sally gripes about the baby getting into her stuff."

    Despite the complaints, the family held the meeting anyway. Both Chuck and George grudgingly attended. After a long discussion, the family finally decided to rotate chores every week. No one was very sympathetic about Sally's complaints. They had heard them so often they tended to ignore her.

Personal Exercise

1. What are the ages of your children? How do you think they would react in a family meeting?

2. What day and time of the week would be good for a meeting for your family?

3. How often do you think your family could productively gather for a family meeting?

4. How long do you think a family meeting should be for your family?

5. What fun activities could you offer at the end of family meetings?

6. Which of your children would be able to take a turn at leading meetings?

7. Do any of your children tend to dominate discussions? (If so, who?)

8. What positive topics and decisions could you discuss at your first family meeting?

9. What problems could you discuss at your first family meeting?

Chapter 8

Behavior Management: Logical Consequences and Positive Reinforcement

BEHAVIOR
MANAGEMENT
— Unrelated Consequences
— Time Out
— Contracts
— Positive Reinforcement
— Logical Consequences
— Family Meetings
COMMUNICATION — Creative Problem-Solving

Unlike most techniques in the previous chapters, behavior management techniques focus on dealing with ongoing problems, rather than preventing them. Behavior management techniques are found higher on the gradient because they are less effective at teaching internal controls. However, these techniques are quite effective at changing behaviors quickly. Use behavior management techniques (a) if a problem is serious, threatening health or property, or (b) if a problem is repetitive. Generally speaking, if prevention and communication techniques do not resolve a problem, then move up the gradient to behavior management techniques.

Many of the techniques in this section originated with the behaviorists, or social learning theorists, such as B. F. Skinner, John Watson, Neal Miller and Albert Bandura. However, *logical consequences* were designed by Alfred Adler and his followers to work without using the rewards or punishments usually found in behaviorist techniques. Behaviorists have adapted logical consequences for use in behavioral management plans.

Contracts (discussed in chapter 9), used widely by behaviorists, are also a therapeutic tool used in Transactional Analysis. *Positive reinforcement* (this chapter) and *time out* (chapter 9) are from behaviorist theories. Some basic behaviorist principles are explained in the section on positive reinforcement.

Inappropriate behaviors cause relationship problems between parents and children. Behavior management techniques improve behavior, leaving the way open for parent and child to rebuild their relationship. When parents use behavior management along with prevention and communication techniques, a very powerful combination results. The behaviorist technique dissolves the offending behavior and the communication or prevention techniques work to resolve the underlying causes.

One of the advantages of discussing theories collectively is to see how the strengths or weaknesses of one theory can be balanced by other, sometimes competing, theories. What behavior management techniques lack in teaching internal controls can be gained by combining them with techniques closer to the beginning of the gradient.

Logical Consequences

Logical consequences are consequences created by the parent *that are related to the child's behavior.* Logical consequences are good teachers of self-discipline.

Three-year-old Melodie was an only child. She played well by herself but found it hard to adjust to playing with other children. When she wanted a toy from another child, she grabbed it away. No matter how much her mother tried to explain that grabbing was impolite, Melodie continued to take toys from other children.

In Melodie's case, there were no consequences occurring naturally that would deter Melodie from grabbing. Melodie's mother decided to artificially create a related consequence that would teach Melodie not to grab. Whenever Melodie took a toy from her playmate, mother gave the toy back to the playmate and set the timer for three minutes. After the timer bell rang, Melodie could play with the toy if she asked for it politely.

Both natural consequences (see chapter 5) and logical consequences are very good at encouraging internal controls and positive self-esteem. The major difference between the two is that *the parent intervenes* in logical consequences. Thus logical consequences can be controlled by the parent, whereas natural consequences can only be accepted or rejected by the parent. A parent can choose a logical consequence that is mild or strong, depending upon the child and the situation. This is why logical consequences are located farther up the discipline gradient, after communication techniques.

CONSEQUENCES: natural, logical and unrelated

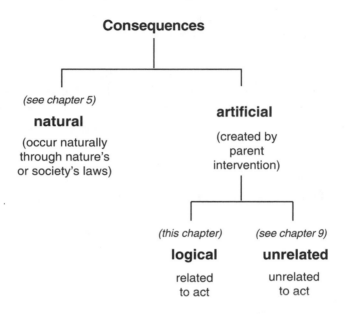

Although Herbert Spencer originally suggested the idea, the principles of logical consequences were developed extensively by Adlerian psychologists. Rudolf Dreikurs, a student and colleague of Alfred Adler, devised many practical applications from Adler's principles.

In his book *Children: The Challenge*, Dreikurs stresses the difference between logical consequences and punishment. Logical consequences are the direct results of children's behaviors. They are not threats (which are not enforced), nor are they accompanied by anger or scoldings. They are simple consequences which relate to the child's actions.

Behaviorist theorists sometimes refer to logical consequences as punishment. However, when used calmly, fairly and reasonably, logical consequences do not fall into the punishment part of the gradient. (Refer to chapter 10 for more information on punishment.)

■ How to use this technique

Consider a troublesome situation. Is there a natural consequence to your child's action? Is the natural consequence acceptable to you? If not, what consequence could be created *that is related to your child's behavior?*

For example, eleven-year-old Jimmy consistently leaves his bicycle in the driveway instead of putting it in the garage where it belongs. There are natural consequences to Jimmy's action—the bicycle might be run over by the car or stolen, or it might rust in the rain. Jimmy's mother and father are not willing to accept the loss of the bicycle—the cost is too high to buy another one, and they do not wish to totally deprive Jimmy of a bicycle to teach him a lesson. Mom and Dad decide to relate the consequence to Jimmy's action by taking away the use of the bicycle for three days.

Other examples of logical consequences:
The child refuses to eat her meal. The parent cleans away the uneaten food. When the child wants snacks before bed, the parent reminds her, "No dinner, no snacks." (Alternative: the child must eat the dinner she refused earlier before she is allowed any snacks.)

The child stays up watching television very late on a school night. The parent restricts television to one program on the following night.

■ Why is this technique valuable?

Logical consequences are powerful teachers. As adults, we experience consequences for most of our actions—learning a skill, being at work on time, having a family, paying a loan. The consequences we experience help us decide whether or not to repeat an action. Although we may or may not listen to others telling us what to do, we usually learn from our direct experiences.

Logical consequences teach responsibility and self-discipline. The child realizes the connection between his actions and the result, which influences his future decisions. Because of the learning that occurs, logical consequences tend to have a lasting effect.

■ Cautions

Be sure the consequences are related to the child's behavior. A child learns more self-discipline from a consequence related to his action than from an unrelated consequence. Taking away television privileges or sending a child to bed may temporarily solve an unrelated problem, but does not show the child a connection between his action and the result. Unrelated consequences tend to impose parental will on the child instead of teaching responsibility.

Mom and Dad could artificially create an unrelated consequence when Jimmy leaves his bike out in the driveway by not allowing him to go to the basketball game Friday night. (See chapter 9 for more information about unrelated consequences.) But if Mom and Dad relate the consequence to the action—by taking away the use of the bicycle for three days—Jimmy is more likely to realize the responsibility of owning a bicycle, and is less likely to feel resentment.

It is best to explain to the child in advance what the logical consequence will be. In this way, the child actually chooses the resulting consequence when he chooses to do the action—this is how responsibility is learned. Explaining consequences in advance avoids the unpleasant surprise which might cause the child to resent the parent.

Sometimes it is not possible to choose a logical consequence in advance of a situation. For example, if a child cheats on an exam or shoplifts, the parents and child together might come up with a logical consequence for the offense that has already occurred.

Logical consequences should be consistent—similar consequences should follow the same behavior every time. *If the adult sometimes fails to follow through, the child learns that sometimes he can get away with it.* He will not learn responsibility for this action, and the unresolved situation will continue.

When Brittany hits her younger brother, her mother usually removes her from play for five minutes. But if Mom is engrossed in a sewing project or reading a book, Brittany knows she will only get a warning. So most of Brittany's hitting occurs when Mom is sewing or reading.

It may take a little while for the child to test the parent enough times to make sure that the consequence always appears. But once the child knows the adult will follow through, the undesirable behavior disappears. The child may need to be reminded occasionally, but will not have to relearn the lesson.

Logical consequences should occur as soon as possible after the event. This is especially true for younger children. If a preschooler cannot play cooperatively with a friend today, it is better to have the friend go home immediately, rather than to say the friend cannot come again next week. An older child or teen can understand consequences that come somewhat later after the action. But the later the consequence arrives, the less potential it has to teach responsibility.

If you deprive a child of something important to him, the amount of time the deprivation lasts should be reasonable. Taking Jimmy's bike away for two months because he left it in the driveway will cause resentment instead of self-discipline. Ignoring a toddler who pulled mom's hair is effective if done for a short time, but will be bewildering and upsetting if mom won't talk to him for half an hour.

Do not deprive a child of something really crucial to him. If your child has been looking forward all year to the state fair with great anticipation, don't take away going to the fair as a consequence of behavior. The crushing reality of missing the fair will overshadow any learning experience and will erode the relationship between you and your child. Choose a different consequence for the undesirable behavior, and use the fair as a time to foster positive relationships.

Choose consequences you can live with. You may not want to ground your teen for four weeks because you don't want your grumpy teen around you that much (see chapter 9 for more on grounding). You may choose not to assign extra chores because you don't have the time to supervise them. You may decide that canceling the family's dinner out will disappoint too many people. It is better to choose different consequences rather than to resent your child for creating extra problems for you.

▣ When to use this technique

Use logical consequences if a situation does not have a naturally occurring consequence. When Mason demands candy from the little kids on the block, no one resists. They meekly give him their candy or lunch treats when he demands it. There is no natural consequence that teaches Mason not to continue this behavior. (As a logical consequence,

Mason's parents could require Mason to use his own money to repay the children for the treats he took.)

Use logical consequences if the natural consequences to a situation are not acceptable. We would not want to use natural consequences to teach three-year-old Rebecca to stay away from matches. We would not choose natural consequences to teach a child to stay out of the street or to refrain from teasing animals. (As a logical consequence for teasing animals, parents could require a child to help a friend care for a pet, or to help a veterinarian for an afternoon.)

Use logical consequences if a child is not influenced by a natural consequence. Cora may not care that her little brother won't play with her when she calls him names. Or Jason may not mind wearing rumpled or soiled clothing that he threw on the floor two days ago.

Sometimes it is just not possible to find a related consequence for a child's action. If so, choose a different discipline technique to deal with the situation. For Jason (in the paragraph above), perhaps hanging up his school clothes is a chore that needs to be done before he is allowed to go out to play (see "Grandma's Rule," chapter 9).

Logical Consequences

1. Choose a consequence that is related to the child's action.
2. If possible, describe the consequence to the child in advance.
3. Always follow through (unless there are unusual circumstances).
4. The consequence should occur as soon as possible after the event.
5. If a period of deprivation is chosen, it should be reasonable in length.
6. Do not deprive children of events that carry great significance.
7. Choose consequences you (the parent) can live with.

■ Ages of children

Logical consequences work very well for children of all ages after infancy. Even an older baby can learn from consequences. If he pulls mom's hair, she turns sharply away from him; if he throws his food, dinner is ended. Toddlers and preschoolers learn many rules through consequences: what happens if they hit someone, throw a toy, make a mess. Logical consequences effectively enforce rules for school-age children and teens.

EXERCISES

Logical Consequences

Practical Exercise

Name a logical consequence for each of the following situations.

1. The child will not stay away from the hot stove while mother is cooking dinner.

2. The child allows her room to become messy and dirty.

3. The child frequently neglects to walk his dog.

4. The teen comes home half an hour late for curfew.

5. The child hits his sister.

6. The child shoplifts.

7. The child dawdles during dressing and eating breakfast, and frequently misses the bus. Dad drives him to school.

8. The teen borrows mom's scarf and loses it.

9. The child refuses to change out of her school clothes after school.

10. The child enjoys baking, but leaves a mess afterward.

Personal Exercise

Describe a situation with your child that you would like to modify by using logical consequences.

1. Undesirable behavior:

2. What would the natural consequences be for this behavior?

3. Are these natural consequences acceptable to you?

4. What logical consequence could you use for this behavior?

5. How do you think your child would respond to this consequence?

Positive Reinforcement Systems

"Catch the child being good," say the behaviorists or social learning theorists. Behaviorists believe that children's behavior is learned through interactions with their environment. Actions which are rewarded, or *reinforced,* will tend to be repeated. Behavior which is not rewarded, or *ignored,* will tend to disappear.

Behaviorists tell us that adult attention is one of the strongest motivators, or reinforcers, for a child's behavior. If a child cannot obtain her parent's attention in a positive way, she will resort to getting her parent's attention in a negative manner. In *How to Discipline With Love*, Dr. Fitzhugh Dodson describes the "Law of the Soggy Potato Chip." Dodson says children prefer a crisp potato chip to a soggy one, but they will be satisfied with a soggy one if no crisp chip is available. In other words, children prefer positive attention from parents. But if positive attention is not available, they will settle for negative attention.

Behaviorists believe that parents often unknowingly encourage negative actions by giving attention to children's undesirable behaviors. That is, parents encourage unpleasant behavior in their children when they threaten, scold and spank them, because children consider punishment better than being ignored. In effect, the parent is programming the child to behave inappropriately in order to receive attention.

Positive reinforcement occurs when a parent offers positive rewards to a child as incentive to change her behavior. Positive reinforcement can be as simple as a giving a smile and a hug when your child does something well.

On a more complicated level, a behavioral plan or positive reinforcement system can be designed for a particular child or group of children. A reinforcement system is a plan to change behavior by combining *positive reinforcement* (for desired behavior) with either *ignoring* or *consequences* (for undesirable behavior).

For example, eight-year-old Robbie Smith had a hard time controlling his anger. When he was denied his wishes, he often struck out, hitting his mother or his younger sister Lynn. His mother was weary and upset about the constant confrontations. Often their fights ended in Robbie shouting "I hate you!" and running to his room, slamming the door. Mrs. Smith would end up in tears.

After consulting with a behavioral counselor, Robbie's mother targeted Robbie's hitting in anger as the behavior she wished to change. After observing and recording his behavior for one week, she decided to offer Robbie a sticker for every afternoon he played cooperatively and did not hit anyone. On Saturdays and Sundays he could earn three stickers (one for morning, one for afternoon and one for evening).

When he had earned eight stickers, he could trade them in for a meal with Mom at his favorite restaurant. Since Mrs. Smith felt she could not ignore Robbie's hitting when it did occur, she planned to give him a time out whenever he hit someone. Mrs. Smith explained the system to Robbie. Robbie was excited about trying for the stickers and dinner out with Mom.

The combination of rewards and time out worked. The first few days Robbie didn't hit at all. On the third day, he forgot about the reward system and hit Lynn. Mother gave him a time out. Robbie was not very happy, but he did not hit again for several more days. Even though he did not have a perfect record, he was able to earn eight stickers by the end of the week. Robbie had a good time with his mother on their dinner out, and asked if next week he could work toward a roller-skating session. His mother agreed. In one week, Robbie's hitting had dropped from an average of 17 hits per week down to 3 hits in one week. The following week, he only hit once.

In addition to positive reinforcement systems, behaviorists sometimes suggest behavioral systems in which points or rewards can be taken away (instead of earned), or systems in which the "reward" is a *decrease* of something negative. I do not recommend these negative reinforcement systems, because personal experience—as well as the experience of many families we have worked with—has convinced me that negative reinforcement systems do not work nearly as well as positive reinforcement. Negative reinforcement systems tend to discourage children and sometimes prevent them from succeeding at a behavioral plan.

Positive reinforcement, however, has a beneficial influence on children's self-esteem as well as their behavior, and usually improves parent-child relationships as the negative behavior changes. Positive reinforcement techniques have the additional advantage of being able to work when almost everything else has been tried.

The section on positive reinforcement is divided into four parts. The first part describes basic positive reinforcement techniques and general guidelines for establishing a behavioral reinforcement plan.

The remaining three parts—praise, star charts, and planned ignoring—discuss in greater depth three commonly used reinforcement techniques.

General guidelines for positive reinforcement

▓ How to use this technique

There are two parts to using positive reinforcement:

1. Ignore the child when he behaves inappropriately, unless:

- it is harmful to the child or someone else,
- it is destructive of property, or
- it is very annoying and difficult to ignore.

(Use different techniques such as logical consequences or time out with behavior too destructive or too undesirable to ignore.)

Ignoring negative behavior eliminates what a misbehaving child can usually count on—attention from the parent. If the parent is able to consistently ignore a particular behavior, eventually it disappears.

2. Offer positive reinforcement (rewards) when the child is doing what you want him to do.

Reinforcements, or rewards, come in different sizes and flavors:

Examples of Positive Reinforcements

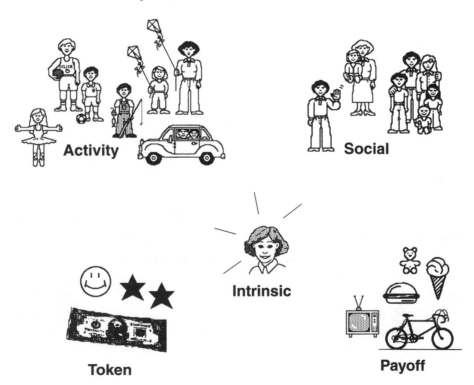

Activity

Social

Token

Intrinsic

Payoff

Social reinforcement includes praise (discussed separately), smiles, attention and hugs. For example, Dad praises three-year-old Jeremiah when he plays cooperatively with the baby (*before* he becomes restless and takes away the baby's toys). Dad gives Cindi a hug when she brings home a project from school.

Activity reinforcement includes any activity rewarding to the child, especially one that includes the parent. For example, if Barry asks for things politely (instead of whining) throughout the morning, he and his mother take a walk to the park after lunch. If Lily picks up her toys during the week, Dad takes her to the movies on Friday night. Activity rewards are particularly valuable because they not only serve as reinforcement, but also offer an opportunity to spend time together, thus strengthening relationships.

Token reinforcement uses tokens (symbols or devices) that can be traded for activities or material rewards (payoffs). Money is a token reinforcement—we modify our behaviors (such as taking a job) to receive money to exchange for other things we want or need. Star charts (discussed separately) are an example of token reinforcement—stars or stickers are collected on a chart for certain desired behaviors. When the child has collected a predetermined amount, he can trade them in for an activity or material reward.

Material rewards, or payoffs, are actual physical rewards such as food, toys or clothes. If Janice finishes her homework before 7 p.m., mother gives her a cupcake. If Christopher gets all As this quarter, Dad will buy him a new bicycle. Material payoffs encourage immediate motivation. But material payoffs are the hardest to wean a child away from. The other categories of reinforcement are less likely to produce a "what's in it for me?" attitude from the child.

Intrinsic reinforcement is the good feeling a child gets inside when he does something well. Intrinsic reinforcement is the goal of positive reinforcement techniques. Children who are trapped in negative self-esteem cycles may rarely, if ever, experience intrinsic reinforcement, since they seem bent on following negative scripts. However, when these children's behaviors are shaped in positive ways by external rewards, intrinsic reinforcement also begins to grow, sometimes for the first time.

I worked at a school where the teachers and other staff joined together in an effort to help a young kindergartner with many social and emotional problems. The staff consistently reinforced any positive behaviors they saw, using consequences and time outs when necessary. The teachers created class-wide and school-wide opportunities where the boy could shine in positive ways, such as helping with the school flag. By the second grade, this child's social behavior was that of an average well-adjusted second-grader. I remember seeing his proud face during a public assembly, where he presented an award to a visitor. The external reinforcement created by this group of concerned adults eventually resulted in positive feelings the young boy could experience himself. At the assembly, intrinsic reinforcement was evident in his posture and shining face.

When using positive reinforcement, follow these guidelines:

1. Make a plan in advance. Decide what specific behavior(s) you would like to change. Decide exactly what reward will be offered. Behavioral scientists suggest observing the child for a period of time and keeping a record of how often and when the targeted behavior occurs. Look for what is currently reinforcing the behavior. Is the child gaining attention from other adults or peers?

The next step is to create a plan which targets particular behaviors and describes specific rewards. In most cases, the adult prepares the child by explaining in advance what reward can be gained for a specific behavior, and how undesirable behaviors will be handled. Occasionally the child is not involved in the preparation, such as in the case of a very young child who will be socially reinforced for playing cooperatively.

Behaviorists suggest keeping track of behaviors not only to prepare a plan, but also after the new system is implemented. By tallying reinforcements and behaviors, the adult can tell how effectively the new system is working, or can come up with strategies to make it work more effectively.

Although results are less consistent, positive reinforcement can be used spontaneously. For example, Jack and Marie were so orderly and responsive at the library puppet show that their mother decided to stop for ice cream afterward as a treat.

2. Be specific. Explain exactly what must be done in order to receive the reward. Your definition of cleaning her room is probably different from your child's definition. Rather than, "If you clean your room, you'll get a treat," state clearly what you expect. "Put the books away neatly in the bookshelf, hang up your clothes, and put away toys in the closet."

Describe the reward clearly. What if you produce the treat, but your child doesn't want it and feels cheated? It is better to clearly arrange the award in advance. "When you are finished, you may have a brownie," or "We'll walk to the library for story time."

3. State expected behavior positively instead of negatively. It is easier for the child if you tell her to *do* something, rather than to *refrain from* doing something. Tell her "please walk," instead of "don't run." Tell him "hang up your coat," instead of "don't throw your coat on the floor."

A *competing behavior* is something that cannot be done at the same time as the behavior you want changed. For example, a child cannot ask politely while she is whining. So "asking politely" is the competing behavior for whining. "Talking quietly" is the competing behavior for shouting. "Playing cooperatively" is the competing behavior for fighting with siblings.

To state behaviors positively, tell the child to do the competing behavior (usually the opposite) of the behavior you wish to change.

4. Reward as soon as possible after the behavior occurs. A payoff is most powerful when it can be given immediately after the action you want to reinforce. The younger the child, the more important it is to reinforce quickly. Young children rarely understand or learn from delayed rewards or consequences. When she finishes making her bed, the preschooler is ready for the promised story. As soon as he finishes using the potty, the toddler is ready for his sticker.

As children grow older, their ability to wait for rewards increases. A second-grader can probably wait for Saturday to go roller-skating. A sixth-grader can wait a few weeks for dance classes to start. A teen can probably wait for a semester for a shopping spree or a vacation. But even with older children, greater learning occurs when the reward is given closer to the required behaviors.

5. To teach a new behavior, reward every time until the behavior is learned. After a behavior is learned, *intermittent reinforcement* is the strongest way to encourage the learned behavior.

An example of the strength of intermittent reinforcement can be shown by a behaviorist experiment with laboratory rats. Continuous reinforcement was used to teach a new behavior: the rats learned that pressing a lever would release food into their cages.

Once the behavior was learned, the scientists divided the rats into three groups. The first group was given food whenever they pressed the lever. The rats in this group pressed the lever only when they were hungry. In the second group, the levers in the rats' cages never released food, no matter how often they were pressed. As expected, those rats soon stopped pressing their levers at all.

The rats in the third group were provided with levers that periodically released food into the cage. The rats learned that food would eventually come if they kept pressing the bar. These rats pressed their levers continuously.

Studies with children confirm the power of intermittent reinforcement. Since it has been found to be such a strong factor, behaviorists caution against accidentally using intermittent reinforcement to reinforce *unwanted* behaviors. For example, occasionally giving in to whining actually reinforces the whining. The child learns to whine harder and longer to get what she wants.

On the positive side, however, intermittent reinforcement is helpful in weaning children from external reward systems. Because children know that *sometimes* their actions will produce rewards, they are likely to continue those actions. At the same time, they are growing in personal pride, or intrinsic reinforcement, which eventually takes the place of external rewards.

6. Each behavior plan should be structured for success. If a behavior plan is too difficult, a child will give up.

(a) Don't try to change too much at once. It is best to choose one behavior to start with, not three or four. Trying to change too many behaviors at once is difficult and confusing. You may want to choose a less significant behavior before working on a more difficult one. In this way, the child is introduced to the idea of reinforcement with less at stake, and he has a greater chance of success.

(b) Leave room for mistakes. If there are ten chances to earn stickers in one week, and your child must earn all ten stickers to go swimming with dad on Saturday, what happens if she earns nine? Disappointment, loss of self-esteem and less desire to try again. Instead, require seven or eight stickers (out of ten chances) for the desired re-

ward. When the child experiences success, she will be eager to continue.

(c) Break large tasks into steps. If a task is too difficult for a child to learn all at once, reward the first step until that behavior is learned. Then reward the next step, and the next, until the full behavior is learned. A toddler who is ready for toilet-training might receive a sticker just for sitting on the potty. After he has learned to sit on the potty, he might receive one sticker if he urinates in the potty, and two stickers if he does a bowel movement in the potty. The next step would be to reward him for keeping his diapers or underpants dry during the day in addition to using the potty successfully. Keeping dry at night, which is the hardest task (sometimes not successfully achieved for years), would be saved for last.

7. *When the child has learned the desired action* and performs it from internal satisfaction, rewards can be saved for special times.

Intermittent reinforcement, as explained earlier, is ideal for weaning a child away from a plan of consistent rewards. A behavioral plan can be ended by telling the children that they are doing so well that a reward system isn't really necessary any more, but occasional rewards will still be available in appreciation for their continued good work.

■ Why is this technique valuable?

Positive reinforcement works well with children who do not respond to other techniques. Systems of reinforcement are used in many (if not most) institutions today, including hospitals for the mentally ill and prisons. Reinforcement (especially when coupled with logical consequences) is the fastest way to change undesirable behavior.

Positive reinforcement systems focus on behavior. They do not try to determine reasons for actions, nor do they try to examine or change emotions. But because they are so helpful at changing difficult behaviors, they often set the stage for emotional changes as well. By easing difficult or repetitive situations, they remove obstacles to positive parent-child relationships and raise self-esteem.

Although positive reinforcement has become very popular in today's society, some theorists (notably the Adlerians) disagree with the behaviorists. Positive reinforcement relies heavily on external controls. It is not as effective at teaching internal controls as the techniques closer to the beginning of the gradient. Also, children may depend on the motivation provided by external rewards unless they are helped to find internal motivation. I recommend that parents who are using positive reinforcement systems with their children simultaneously try other techniques closer to the beginning of the gradient, such as active listening, "I messages" and creative problem-solving. In this way, self-discipline grows while behavior is changing.

Generally speaking, positive reinforcement is very effective at quickly changing behaviors, but needs help from other techniques to promote internal change and long-term results.

■ Cautions

Don't reinforce inappropriate behavior with negative attention. Remember that when an action is followed by reinforcement—even the soggy potato chip of negative attention—the action is likely to be repeated. Darrell, seven years old, insists on staying up late at night. His parents struggle with him every night for more than an hour before he will go to bed. An hour's worth of attention—even negative—is a strong reinforcer for Darrell's resistance.

Often when children engage in annoying but not dangerous behaviors, we react intermittently. Sometimes we put up with it. Sometimes—especially on the days when we experience more stress in our lives—we object. By intermittently responding to the behavior, behaviorists would say we are strongly reinforcing negative behavior. The solution? React as consistently as possible, and explain your reasons whenever you change or relax the rules.

Ignore negative behaviors while simultaneously reinforcing positive behaviors. Jerome, age 4, often captured Dad's attention by jumping on the furniture. Jerome would stop obediently when Dad shouted at him, but within a few minutes after Dad was busy elsewhere, Jerome would start jumping again. After observing this pattern, Dad began to ignore Jerome's jumping. He also began to chat with Jerome periodically when Jerome was sitting on the couch. Within two weeks, Jerome's jumping had almost disappeared. Children who consistently seem to search for negative attention respond very well when they begin to receive positive attention at other times. In many cases, the negative behaviors disappear without further discipline.

Choose rewards desirable to the child. Take your child's special likes into account when you decide on a reward. What activities does your child enjoy doing? What hobbies does she have? What possessions does she treasure? If a reinforcement plan is not working, it may be because your child does not value the reward as much as you thought she would. Include her in the selection process.

Distinguish between feelings and actions. Actions are outward, observable events—such as whether the chores were done or not. Feelings belong to the child. Reinforce specific, observable actions, not feelings. In other words, reinforce your child when she takes out the garbage, whether or not she grumbles along the way.

We may not like getting up early every morning to get to work on time—in fact, we may grumble about it. But accepting responsibility means we do get up and get there on time, no matter what our personal feelings are. In the same way, children have a right to their own feelings, even though they may need to perform certain actions.

Don't offer rewards for stopping negative behaviors. Don't say, "Stop fighting, and I'll treat you to ice cream." A short-term reward used to stop a negative behavior actually *reinforces* the negative behavior. I remember one important long-distance phone call when my three little children swamped me with questions and demands. Desperate, I practically threw a box of chocolate chip cookies at them. I made it through that particular phone call. But when the next important call came, all three of them were ready. They knew just what to do to get the cookies!

Instead, reinforce positive behavior. "I'll give you each a cookie if you can be quiet while I'm on the phone." Let children accomplish that behavior for a suitable time frame before giving them the reward.

Don't give up too soon. One of the benefits of positive reinforcement is how quickly it can change behavior. However, to thoroughly learn a new behavior, one psychologist estimates that 30 to 40 time outs (discussed later in this chapter) and 50 to 100 positive reinforcements are needed.

On the other hand, overusing positive reinforcement systems (that is, using them for minor daily infractions) tends to create the "what's in it for me?" syndrome. Small rewards lose their appeal, and larger and more expensive rewards are required for motivation. Use positive reinforcement to create change, then take a break from it and use other techniques listed earlier on the gradient to encourage self-discipline.

Positive Reinforcement

1. Reward behavior you wish repeated.
2. Ignore behavior you wish eliminated (or use logical consequences).
3. Don't accidently reinforce negative behavior.
4. Choose rewards the child wants.
5. Wean the child through intermittent reinforcement.
6. Design your program for success (break large tasks into steps).

■ When to use this technique

Positive reinforcement works well for any kind of behavioral changes. But because positive reinforcement is higher on the gradient—thus less effective at promoting internal controls—I recommend using this technique when

- *a problem is serious,* that is, it is dangerous to the child or to persons and things around her; or
- *a (less serious) problem consistently recurs* and cannot be eliminated by prevention or communication techniques.

■ Ages of children

Positive reinforcement works for most children and adults, but some types work better at certain ages. *Token reinforcement* works very well with preschool and school-age children. School-age children particularly enjoy the counting and organizational aspects to token systems, such as star charts. Token systems (with the exception of money!) are less effective with teens (who are interested in other things) or with very young children (who have a hard time understanding them).

Social reinforcers and *material rewards* work well with all ages. Very young children respond best to social reinforcers and material rewards because they are liked, easily understood and usually offered immediately after a desired behavior.

Activity reinforcers work best for toddlers, preschoolers and school-age children. Teens tend to be involved with their peers and less likely to think of family activities as rewards. Desired activity reinforcers for teens are often activities with their peers.

Intrinsic rewards cannot be given out by adults. But adults can encourage intrinsic satisfaction by structuring behavioral plans to achieve success.

EXERCISES

Positive Reinforcement

Practical Exercise

Identify the mistakes in the following positive reinforcement scenarios. What would be a better response?

1. Rachel, age 3, received a sticker if she could get ready for pre-school on time. When she earned five stickers, Dad would take her to the movies. Rachel was getting discouraged because two weeks had passed and she had only earned three stickers.

2. Lauren's father told her that if she shaped up and did her chores more often, he would bring her a surprise.

3. Jimmy, age 4, wouldn't be quiet during the church service. Mother told him he could have a stick of gum if he would stop disturbing the people in front of them.

4. Shane, 11, had difficulty keeping his grades above Ds. Mother promised him a television for his room if he could improve his grades.

5. Dad promised to take Sarah, age 15, to a family movie if she would help with the dishes every night for two weeks.

6. Shannon, age 9, stopped biting her nails. Dad was so pleased he said they would redecorate her room next summer.

Personal Exercise

1. What age is your child?

2. What activities does he/she enjoy doing? (Include activities shared by mom or dad.)

3. What hobbies does your child enjoy? What possessions? What social reinforcement does he/she respond to?

4. Which of your child's behaviors do you particularly like?

5. Do you reinforce any of those behaviors with positive reinforcement? (Describe.)

6. Which of your child's behaviors do you particularly dislike or want to change?

7. Choose one of the behaviors in #6 that you would like to change through positive reinforcement. Describe the behavior you would rather have (the competing behavior). Use specific language in a positive statement (what to *do*, not what to *refrain from doing*):

8. What reinforcement can you offer for this behavioral change?

9. When and how often would the reinforcement occur? Who would give it?

10. Can you ignore the undesirable behavior completely if it occurs? If not, choose a consequence for the undesirable behavior.

11. Observe your child for one week before you try any changes. Record how often and when the targeted (undesirable) behavior occurs.

12. Now discuss your reinforcement plan with your child. Try it for one week. Record how often and when the targeted (undesirable) behavior occurs. Record reinforcements and responses. Record the number of consequences and responses.

13. At the end of one week, evaluate your plan. Is it working? What behaviors have changed? What rewards have been earned? How do you and your child feel about it?

Praise

Praise is expressing approval or admiration. Behaviorists view praise as a social reinforcer (see previous section). When a child's action is praised, the action will tend to be repeated. Praise also influences a child's self-esteem and boosts confidence.

The previous section on positive reinforcement explains the use of social reinforcement. A few specific points are presented in this section to help parents use praise more effectively.

▇ How to use this technique

1. *Praise should be specific.* Specific praise helps the child determine exactly what was well done so it can be repeated or improved upon. It also helps the child feel that the praise was sincere. For example, Bill's mother praised her son's modern artwork by commenting on the colors and the patterns. Bill thought, "Mom's not just saying something nice. She really likes the colors and the design."

On a more subtle level, specific praise admires the task, not the child. Admiring the *task* helps the child feel confident about his abilities. Admiring the *child* can build expectations that may hinder the child later. For example, constantly praising Celeste for being "Mother's little helper" might eventually encourage Celeste to build her identity around always being a helper, when in fact she is much more than that. Children who are constantly praised about being "the brain" might build educational expectations of themselves that are nearly impossible to meet. However, praising the *task* gives children feelings of accomplishment which, in turn, raise their self-esteem. With positive self-esteem, the child feels even more confident and willing to try more new things. It's a rewarding cycle.

Instead of: "Thanks. You are my best helper."

try this: "Thank you for picking up the toys and sweeping the floor."

Instead of: "You are a good athlete. I'm proud of you."

try this: "I really like the way you handle the ball. You move confidently and quickly without pushing or shoving. I'm proud of you."

2. Just as with other types of positive reinforcement, *praise should be offered as soon as possible after the event.* Very young children need to be praised immediately after their accomplishment. Praising them the next day or week is meaningless, because the event is too far away for them to get in touch with it. Although older children can appreciate praise even after the event has passed, the sooner the praise is offered, the more effective it is and the better it feels.

3. *Praise your child for steps along the way to a goal.* Perhaps a better name for this type of praise is *encouragement.* All children need encouragement, especially those children who currently don't meet many

goals. If only the end result is praised, children may feel that the end result is all that matters. In reality, effort and methods may be even more important. Encouraging the steps toward a goal is an excellent way to help the child meet more goals. Alfred Adler and his followers consider encouragement (or discouragement) as a major motivation for children. Rudolf Dreikurs' book, *Children: the Challenge,* and Michael Popkin's book, *Active Parenting,* describe additional ways to encourage children.

> *Instead of:* "This is a great report." (after the project is done)
> (praise)
>
> *how about:* "I see you are using library books to support
> (encouragement) your ideas. It's not easy to write a good report.
>   Looks like you've got a good start." (in progress)

Parents often tend to rescue a floundering child. It is actually more beneficial to offer encouragement to the child along with helpful suggestions. Encouragement appreciates a child's effort by recognizing the difficulty of the task.

> *Instead of:* "Here, let me help you thread that needle."
> (rescue)
>
> *how about:* "Threading a needle is a hard job. It helps if you
> (encouragement) cut the end of the thread and wet it."

Rescuing a child tends to give him the feeling that he was not competent to handle the task. Encouragement points out that the child is working hard at a task which is difficult for others as well as himself.

■ Why is this technique valuable?

Praise is an excellent positive reinforcer. When a child is praised for doing something well, he is more likely to do it again.

Praise helps children feel good about themselves; it helps build intrinsic reinforcement. Children feel successful when they are praised, which leads toward more success and positive self-esteem.

Encouragement helps build motivation as well as self-esteem. When children are encouraged during the process, they are more likely to try the process again in other situations.

▉ Cautions

1. Don't use praise too much. Too much praise becomes commonplace, and is soon ignored. Children assume that's just the way dad talks, or that mom says that about everything. The purpose of praise—to help the child feel special or feel she has done something particularly well—is lost. Don't praise your child constantly for everything she does. Praise her when she does something very well, when she shows great effort, when she needs encouragement, or when she takes a step—however small—in the direction you'd like her to go.

2. Be sincere. Your children know if you don't mean it, so don't say it unless you do. Say something else that you do mean—such as "my, that's unusual" or "that's creative." Save your praise for another occasion when it will mean more.

3. Try not to couple praise with a negative comment. "Your room sure looks great; now why can't you keep it that way?" Slipping in a little lecture negates the effect of the praise. Praise is meant to make the child feel special, so he will want to repeat the action for his own feelings of self-worth.

A positive comment can soften a criticism, but realize that it will have a much different effect than praise by itself. An "I message" (chapter 6) is a good way to phrase criticism.

▉ When to use this technique

Praise your child often, but not constantly. Praise her when she does something very well, when she shows great effort or when she needs encouragement.

Use *encouragement* frequently. If a child is having a hard time learning how to tie her shoes, explain that learning to tie a knot is a difficult task. Appreciate her effort, her persistence or her improvement. Acknowledging the difficulty of the task shows respect for the child's struggle and is more beneficial to the child's self-esteem than rescuing her ("I'll do it for you, honey").

▉ Ages of children

Children of all ages can appreciate and learn from praise.

Praise

1. Be specific.
2. Praise as soon as possible after the event.
3. Offer encouragement along the way to a goal.
4. Don't overuse praise.
5. Be sincere.
6. Try not to couple praise with a negative comment.

EXERCISES

Praise

Practical Exercise

What is wrong with each response below? How would you change it to make it better?

1. To Andy, age 8: "I'm glad you washed your hands; I wish you would do it more often."
   Better response:

2. To Cheryl, age 5: "That's a very nice picture."
   Better response:

3. To Elizabeth, age 7 (before swimming class): "Why are you nervous? You swam very well last week."
   Better response:

4. To Randall, age 4: "Those are pretty worms you found."
   Better response:

5. To Candy, age 10: "I'm glad you got Bs on your report card, but remember your sister gets mostly As."
    Better response:

6. To Brett, age 13, "You're doing a good job with your chores."
    Better response:

7. To Jackson, age 16 (after haircut): "Wow, you look human again."
    Better response:

8. To Carol, age 9: "You are our family's peacemaker."
    Better response:

9. To Jimmy, age 3 (before bed): "I liked it a few days ago when you put on your pajamas without my asking."
    Better response:

10. To Janell, age 4 (viewing a sloppily made bed): "You did a very good job."
    Better response:

Personal Exercise

1. How often do you praise your child daily? weekly?

2. Is it too often? too seldom?

3. How does your child react to praise from you? from others?

4. List the most important behaviors for which you want to praise your child:

5. Choose one activity from the previous question. Write a statement praising the event:

6. List several activities for which your child could use encouragement:

7. Choose one activity from the previous question. Write a statement encouraging your child:

Praise

Star charts and token economies

A star chart is an example of a *token economy*. Tokens are objects that can be traded in for something the child wants. A token economy is a system where tokens are earned by specific behaviors. Tokens are traded in whenever the child earns enough for a reward. A parent may put a bean in a jar every time his children play cooperatively. When the jar is filled, the family plans an outing. Star charts use stars or stickers on a chart to keep track of behaviors. When the chart is filled, the children receive a reward.

■ How to use this technique

Draw (or find) any chart or picture that can be filled with stars or stickers (see examples that follow). For young children, use simple pictures or charts and work on only one behavioral change at a time. For school-age children, list up to four behaviors. Every time the child does the behavior, he chooses a star or sticker to place on the chart. To receive a reward, the child may:

1. fill all the empty spaces with stars (no time limit), *or*
2. fill a percentage of spaces with stars within an allotted time.

Whichever system is used, it should be structured so the child may reach success without a lot of strain. Success brings more success. If a chart is too difficult, the child is likely to give up.

For a Preschooler

The child places one sticker on one star at the end of each day, as long as she has had no time outs that day. When the picture is full (five stickers), the child picks one of several activities with the parent (such as a movie).

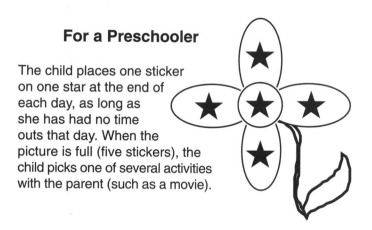

Example for a preschool child:

Maria, three years old, received time outs from her mother if she hit other children, or if she wouldn't obey. Maria's mother decided to try a star chart to positively motivate Maria to change her behavior. Mother drew a simple flower, with places for five stars. Each day that Maria did not get a time out, she received a star for her chart. When five stars were earned (which took seven days, due to two failures), Maria and her mother went swimming together. Maria was delighted with the chart. Her behavior improved dramatically. Maria's mother was also delighted with the chart. Instead of dwelling on the negative, both mother and child were positively motivated. In addition, Maria's mother found herself using more prevention and communication techniques and fewer time outs, because she wanted Maria to be successful with her chart.

For a School-Age Child

	Mon.	Tues.	Wed.	Thurs.	Fri.
Make bed	★				
Hang up clothes					
Play cooperatively with sister	★				
Do homework	★				

3 stars/day = ½ hour extra time before bed at night.
16 stars/week = roller-skating on Saturday.

Example for a school-age child:
Jordan's mother constantly had to remind her son, age 9, to do his homework, make his bed or hang up his clothes. In addition, Jordan tended to make fun of his sister, particularly when he had a bad day at school. Jordan's mother chose to put these four behaviors on a star chart. Concentrating on the school week, she gave Jordan a small incentive each day. If Jordan could earn three out of four stars, he could stay up a half hour later before bed. If he could earn 16 stars out of a possible 20 per school week, Jordan's mother would take him roller-skating on Saturday. Jordan enjoyed keeping track of his activities. Before, his chores had seemed a burden; now they were more like a game. He was delighted to earn extra play time each evening and looked forward to roller-skating on Saturday. Jordan's mother was happy to not have to remind him anymore. In addition, Jordan's little sister asked to have a star chart too, since it looked like so much fun.

Write and rewrite charts according to your creativity and imagination. There are limitless variations on star charts. Today many parents use stickers, rather than stars. Attractive stickers come in all sizes and shapes, including seasonal stickers for holidays. Use any form of chart that works for your children, keeping in mind the cautions listed on the following page.

In addition to star charts, three-dimensional token economies may be used. An empty jar can be filled with beans or pennies or marbles. Each bean is earned by a specific behavior, discussed with the child in advance. When the jar is full, the promised reward is earned. The jar system works very well with groups of children, such as siblings in a family or students in a classroom. Whenever the group as a whole accomplishes the required behavior, another bean goes in the jar. (In some situations, individual members might earn tokens for the whole group.) When the jar is full, the family or the class gets a group reward. For example, if the Smith children play together cooperatively without fighting, Mrs. Smith puts a marble in the jar. When the jar is full, the whole family goes to the zoo.

■ Why is this technique valuable?

School-age children enjoy counting numbers, organizing systems and keeping track of items. Difficult behaviors turn around quickly. Rewards are great motivators, and stickers serve as immediate mini-rewards. Toddler and preschool age children also enjoy star charts, as long as they are simple. Stickers, used in place of stars, are often motivators by themselves.

Trying to eliminate a behavior is often a difficult task. Star charts switch the emphasis from *not doing* the undesirable behavior to *doing* the desirable behavior.

Activity rewards are ideal for star chart goals because they needn't cost much (there are many free outings available, such as playing in the park or going to the library) and they provide opportunities for parents and children to spend time together.

Star charts, filling empty jars and other token systems work well with groups of children, as well as with single children.

■ Cautions

Don't make star charts too long. Toddlers and preschoolers should have only one behavior on a star chart. For school-age children, choose one to four behaviors. If there are more than four behaviors on a chart, parents and children find themselves with complex record-keeping and supervisory checking. It is harder to remember to do all the tasks, plus it is tiring to keep track daily. With these disadvantages, it is easier for a child to fail or to tire of the whole project.

Some systems (usually those involving serious behaviors) allow the adult to take back tokens from the child if rules are violated. However, taking away tokens for undesirable behavior has an important disadvantage: it is easy for the child to become discouraged with the whole system when she is unable to earn sufficient tokens to cash in for a reward. *I strongly advise against using token or point systems where tokens or points are taken away.* In my experience, they have a much higher likelihood of failure. If a consequence for undesirable behaviors is necessary, a separate technique can be used concurrently (such as logical consequences or time out).

Evaluate after one or two weeks. Star charts and token economies are effective ways to change behavior quickly, but they can become boring or stressful if they go on for too long. When your child has learned the behavior, you can wean him from the star chart by explaining that since he is doing so well, the chart is not needed anymore. But remember to offer intermittent rewards for the learned behaviors to encourage the child to continue doing them.

Follow other reinforcement guidelines (see previous section on positive reinforcement), such as choosing a reward desirable to your child, reinforcing with stickers or other tokens as soon as possible after the desired behavior, breaking complex behaviors into steps (and rewarding the steps until the whole behavior is learned), preparing the child in advance, describing behaviors and rewards specifically, and designing token systems to achieve success.

■ When to use this technique

Use star charts to motivate children (a) with serious problems, or (b) with repetitive problems difficult to solve.

Chores also fit well on star charts. Four chores for a school-age child is the maximum. One or two chores is a good number for a preschooler.

■ Ages of children

School-age children respond best to star charts. They particularly enjoy systems, numbers, organization and keeping track.

Preschoolers respond well to simplified star charts. Some toddlers enjoy very simple star charts. Although babies respond well to other types of positive reinforcement, they are too young to understand star charts or other token economies.

Teens are generally not interested in star charts or token economy systems. A reinforcement system for teens that works very well is the *contract* (discussed in the next chapter). However, the concept of reinforcement can be molded in other ways to fit teen needs. One parent—a music teacher—was very upset when her 14-year-old daughter Jeri decided not to continue her enrollment in band upon entering high school. She asked her daughter, "What can I give you that would persuade you to stay in band this year?"

Jeri thought about it for several days and then gave her mother the answer: "I'd like to have two holes put in each ear for pierced earrings." Jeri's mother agreed, the ears were pierced, and Jeri stayed in band. Several years later, Jeri had not only continued to play in concert band, but was intrinsically motivated to get up early to play in the 6:30 a.m. jazz band rehearsals before school.

EXERCISES

Star Charts and Token Economies

Practical Exercise

Design a star chart for the following example:

Aaron, age 7, hates to go to bed at night. He delays putting his pajamas on and brushing his teeth. He loves bedtime stories, however, and pleads, "Just one more; just one more!" After his mom or dad leave the room, he finds many excuses to get up again: needing a glass of water, using the bathroom or wanting another good-night hug. He argues at length with his parents about going to sleep. They check on him and find him playing with toys in bed. Aaron loves reading and books. Aaron is not very neat, however. Books and toys are frequently left lying around the living room and kitchen. Stacks of books sit on his bedroom floor.

Design a token system (such as the empty jar system) for the following example:
Jasmine, Carla, Peter and Kim—all preschoolers—spend after-
noons together at Jasmine's mother's house, while the other three
mothers work part-time. The children love to play in the nearby
park or walk to the library with Jasmine's mother, Mrs. Cane.
Their favorite treat is when Mrs. Cane makes pizza. The four
children usually play well together, but lately have begun arguing
about toys and refusing to share. Each child reacts in a different
way: Jasmine grabs toys away from the other children, Carla
pouts, Peter hits and Kim whines to Mrs. Cane.

Personal Exercise

1. Is your child between the ages of 2½ and 11? (If not, modify
   the following steps to fit the age of your child.)

2. What activities does he/she enjoy doing? What hobbies does
   he/she enjoy? What possessions?

3. Which of your child's behavior(s) would you like to change?

4. Choose one or more of the behaviors in #3 above. Design a
   star chart or other token system for these behaviors. What are
   the rewards? How many possible tokens (stars, stickers) can
   your child earn? How many tokens are required to achieve a
   reward? What is the time frame? Be sure to keep your token
   system very simple if your child is young.

5. Try the star chart or other token system with your child for one week. Be sure to prepare your child by explaining the system clearly. Evaluate after one week. What positive things happened? What negative things happened? What can you do to improve this system?

Planned ignoring

Planned ignoring is ignoring a child's undesirable behavior with the purpose of decreasing and eliminating it. Planned ignoring is called *extinction* by the behaviorists when it is used by itself.

Planned ignoring is useful for undesirable behaviors that are not too serious or too persistent. It can be used by itself, or combined very effectively as part of positive reinforcement (covered earlier in this chapter).

▇ How to use this technique

Make a plan in advance. Choose a behavior you wish to eliminate by ignoring. For several days or one week, record how often and when this behavior occurs. Prepare children by telling them you will no longer respond to this behavior; then begin the ignoring on a particular day.

Do not respond, no matter what, to the behavior. Remember that intermittent reinforcement is the strongest reinforcement (see first part of this chapter). If the parent occasionally responds to the behavior, the child learns he needs to do that behavior even more intensely to achieve a result.

After the ignoring begins, usually the behavior intensifies as the child tries harder to meet his goals. Eventually the child realizes that no matter how hard or how often he tries this behavior, there will be no response from the parent. At this point, the behavior is usually dropped. However, a child may try the behavior again on a different occasion, just to be sure the rules have really changed. If again there is no response, again the behavior stops. Because each child and situation is different, the number of times the child will resurrect the behavior will differ. But eventually the behavior should disappear.

Dustin (6 years) and Brandon (8 years) were in the habit of sitting at the table while Mom was making dinner, demanding snacks the whole time until dinner was ready. Mom sometimes gave in and found snacks for them. At other times, she ordered them out of the kitchen. Even then, they often came back asking for snacks.

Mom decided to ignore their behavior completely with the purpose of eliminating it. She observed them for three days. It didn't seem to matter whether or not she had a snack ready for them—the boys still bothered her while she was making the meal. Mom decided to provide a healthy snack after school each day. Then she explained to the boys that she would no longer respond to additional requests for snacks before dinner.

On the first day, 15 minutes after consuming the after-school snack, the boys came back into the kitchen and sat down at the table. When Mom ignored them, they giggled self-consciously and left the kitchen, remembering what she had said. But a few minutes later they were back at the table asking for more snacks. Mom still ignored them. The boys became even louder. They were still ignored. Finally they left the kitchen until they were called for dinner.

On the second day, Dustin and Brandon followed their mother into the kitchen as soon as she began to make dinner. They asked for snacks; she ignored them. They became louder and louder in their requests. Still their mother ignored them. Finally they looked at each other, shrugged and left the kitchen. They did not come back until shortly before dinner was served.

On the third day, the boys trooped into the kitchen when Mom began making dinner. Almost immediately they remembered that she would not respond to their requests. The boys left the kitchen and did not return until dinner time.

Occasionally in the following days and weeks, Dustin and Brandon would again ask Mom for snacks while she was making dinner. But each time, Mom totally ignored them. Each time they quickly gave up the attempt. After one month, the boys rarely entered the kitchen while Mom was preparing dinner.

Keeping track of the behavior during the process helps the parent understand what is happening. Sometimes it seems as if the ignoring is not working, but the written record shows that the behavior is, in fact, reducing in frequency. If the parents continue to ignore the behavior (and the behavior is not reinforced elsewhere), the child will eventually give up and the behavior will disappear.

Sometimes the written record will point out a hidden reinforcement for the behavior. Kitty (age 4) liked to jump on her parents' bed while Dad was folding the laundry. Dad repeatedly told her to stop. Sometimes she stopped willingly, but usually Dad had to lift her off the bed. Frequently she climbed back on and continued bouncing.

Dad decided to fold the laundry in the living room and totally ignore Kitty's jumping. The record Dad kept showed that the duration of bouncing lessened, but the frequency did not. Kitty enjoyed bouncing on the bed whether Dad was in the room or not. She was receiving reinforcement just from the activity itself. Since Dad could not easily take this reinforcement away, he decided to use a different technique to approach the problem.

■ Why is this technique valuable?

Used by itself, planned ignoring is valuable in eliminating less serious behaviors with little or no confrontation.

In positive reinforcement systems, planned ignoring lessens the attraction of negative behaviors while the parent is using rewards to encourage positive behaviors.

■ Cautions

Planned ignoring is not the best method to deal with serious behaviors, since these behaviors will probably increase before they decrease. In addition, planned ignoring requires more time to eliminate a behavior than some other techniques. If a behavior is potentially dangerous, causing injury to a person or thing, it is better to choose a technique that will modify the behavior in a shorter period of time.

For planned ignoring to work, *the parent or teacher must be able to ignore the behavior at all times.* Intermittent responses actually reinforce the behavior more strongly (see "How to use this technique"). If whining is hard to ignore, parents can indirectly distract the child by beginning an interesting activity that the child joins. However, it is important not to give the child direct attention at this time, because the attention would reinforce the behavior you are trying to extinguish.

If the behavior is very annoying, the adult can leave the room. But if the behavior is so annoying that a parent occasionally breaks down and responds, then it is better not to use planned ignoring for that particular problem.

Be sure to ignore the behavior, and not the child. It is a painful experience for a child to be ignored by his parent. The child should know that he can immediately stop the ignoring by changing his behavior.

■ When to use this technique

Use planned ignoring when you want to eliminate a mild (not dangerous) behavior with minimum confrontation.

Use planned ignoring with a positive reinforcement system to reduce the unwanted behavior while reinforcing the positive behavior with a reward.

Do not use planned ignoring if you are not sure you can totally ignore the child's behavior.

Do not use planned ignoring by itself for serious or dangerous problems, because the behavior tends to increase before decreasing.

■ Ages of children

Planned ignoring can work with any age child. It generally takes a little longer for babies and toddlers to change their behaviors, especially if they do not understand why they are being ignored. However, the lack of attention (reinforcement) will still influence their behaviors.

Explaining to an older child in advance can help shorten the transition time.

Planned Ignoring

1. Use planned ignoring with positive reinforcement when the behavior is not serious.
2. Use planned ignoring by itself only if the behavior is not serious and if you will be able to ignore the behavior *every time* it happens.
3. Realize that the unwanted behavior will probably increase before it decreases.

EXERCISES

Planned Ignoring

Practical Exercise

What is wrong with the following planned-ignoring situations?

1. Mother ignored two-year-old Kristin when she climbed on the furniture. But Kristin didn't stop climbing, and Mother was afraid she would fall.

2. Cameron tended to whine a lot, particularly before lunch and after he woke from his nap. Mom ignored him all morning, but lectured when the whining grew in intensity that afternoon. She ignored him the next day, except for one time when she gave in to his demands for a cookie. Cameron's whining continued.

3. Dad ignored Christopher when he clowned around during the concert. The two girls in the row behind giggled at Christopher, and a boy on the end of the row watched all three. Christopher kept clowning.

4. The teacher decided to ignore Jim's refusal to bring back homework each day.

5. Mom ignored Pam when she tattled on her little sister Brianna. That night at dinner, Mom scolded Brianna in front of Dad and Pam.

Personal Exercise

1. Describe an undesirable behavior you would like to try to eliminate through planned ignoring.

2. Is the behavior too serious or dangerous for this method? (If yes, choose another technique.)

3. Can you ignore the behavior *every* time it happens? (If you can't answer "yes" to this question, don't use planned ignoring for this problem.)

4. Is it possible to leave the room if the problem is hard to ignore while you are present?

5. What other activity can you do that will indirectly interest the child without giving him your direct attention?

Chapter 9

Behavior Management: Contracts, Time Out and Unrelated Consequences

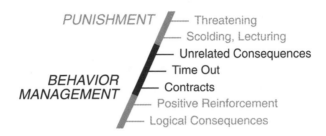

Behavioral Contracts

A behavioral contract is a mutual agreement between parent and child resulting from negotiation. Contracts are written down. Together, parents and child target one or more behaviors to be modified and decide on the rewards to be received as the motivation for change. Sometimes consequences for undesirable behavior are included.

Behavioral contracts work especially well with teens. Teens may get bored with the counting and recording required by star charts, but they tend to be pleased by the negotiation of contracts. Contracts hint at adult status, which most teens look forward to.

Behavioral contracts are listed high on the gradient because they are not the best teachers of internal controls. However, the advantage of mutual negotiation and high appeal to teens makes them attractive discipline techniques. In addition, contracts work very well for children with strong or persistent discipline problems.

Contracts are used as therapeutic tools in transactional analysis as well as in behavioral counseling.

■ How to use this technique

Discuss and negotiate the contract with the child. Creative problem-solving (discussed in chapter 7) is a great way to come up with ideas together. The negotiation process results in a commitment on both sides, sometimes requiring compromise by both parent and child. The commitment is written down, which prevents misunderstanding and arguments later. Each person receives a copy.

Describe behavior and rewards specifically. To decide whether or not the contract terms have been met, it must be possible to observe and count specific behaviors. Actions stated in vague language cannot be easily defined or counted.

For example:
"Sandy will set the table every evening, dust twice a week, and help with the laundry on Saturdays."

is better than:
"Sandy will help Mom around the house."

Suggest positive behaviors rather than listing what should be avoided. The child should agree to *do* something rather than agree *not to do* something. It is much easier to learn new behaviors than to refrain from an old behavior. Results will also be easier to measure.

For example:
"Jimmy will put his toys away each day before eating dinner."

is better than:
"Jimmy will not leave his toys lying around the house."

Be sure the contract is fair. Both parent and child must feel they have made a good deal. If one side feels that the contract is not fair, that person will not have the motivation to follow through.

Design the contract to be successful. It is better not to require perfect scores in the contract, but to leave room for improvement. If the child experiences some success, he is likely to want to continue the contract. If the child cannot reasonably attain his goals, he is likely to lose interest while his self-esteem drops.

A behavioral contract should contain:
- the date the agreement starts and ends
- the behaviors targeted for change
- the reward: what kind, how often, who gives it
- the signatures of involved parties
- a review date
- bonus for exceptional performance (optional)

SAMPLE CONTRACT 1

CONTRACT BETWEEN: Tim Brown   **AND**   Bob Brown

Effective Dates: From Jan. 5, 1999   **to**   Feb. 4, 1999

We, the undersigned, agree to perform the following behaviors:

If Bob attends all   **then**   he may have the car
classes in the   one afternoon each week
school day,   and one weekend night.

BONUS: If all grades are above a "C," Bob may take the car
to school one day a week.

PENALTY: If Bob cuts a class, he will lose his car
privileges for the week.

Date: _____

Signed: _____
  (teen)

_____
  (parent)

This contract will be
reviewed   2   weeks from date
of agreement, on   1/19/99

Follow basic positive reinforcement principles. That is, the reward should be desirable to the child, complicated tasks should be broken into steps, the reward should not be too far in the distant future, and the child should not receive reinforcement from another source (see positive reinforcement section).

Phase out contracts when they no longer seem needed. At the contract ending date:

- the contract may be renewed,
- a new contract may be substituted,
- a new discipline method may be chosen, or
- the contract may be phased out.

If the contract is phased out, continue to provide intermittent positive reinforcement to reinforce the newly learned behavior.

■ Why is this technique valuable?

A contract usually works well with rebellious or difficult children because the mutual respect and negotiation favorably influences their self-esteem, while giving them some personal control.

Contracts provide motivation, especially in the case of children who do not respond well to other discipline techniques.

Contracts are one of the few discipline techniques (especially of those on this end of the gradient) that tend to be very attractive to teens. Teens enjoy the mutual negotiation, the motivation provided by rewards and the adult status suggested by making a contract. Teens also are more likely to accept consequences written into a mutually advantageous contract when they are reluctant to accept them otherwise.

■ Cautions

Try to avoid contracts which give points for good behavior and take away points for bad behavior—they tend to be too discouraging for the child. However, consequences for behaviors can be included, depending on the situation and the child.

Allow the child to grumble or gripe as long as he does the required action in the contract. The child's feelings belong to the child, not the parent, and how the child feels is not part of the contract.

Rewards should always come after children have performed what they promised. Don't allow credit. Once the reward is received, there is little motivation for following through on changes.

Contracts should be made rationally, not emotionally. Think through all aspects of the contract. Don't agree to the terms unless they are logically decided upon. Don't accept or abandon a contract solely because of the way you feel about it.

■ When to use this technique

Use contracts to solve problems with teens when they do not respond to prevention or communication techniques.

Use contracts to help solve problems with younger children if they do not respond to—or are bored with—positive reinforcement systems, and you have already tried prevention and communication techniques.

Use contracts at other times if they seem to approach a problem in a mutually satisfactory way for parent and child. Because contracts are far to the right on the discipline gradient, try combining contracts with other techniques—such as building relationships, "I messages," creative problem-solving or family meetings—that are better at building internal controls.

■ Ages of children

Teens particularly value the adult approach of behavioral contracts. Contracts with teens might last a month, several months or a semester, but long-term contracts should be reviewed after several weeks to make sure the motivation for change is still there.

Children ages 6 to 12 also respond well to contracts. The contracts should be simpler and should last for shorter periods of time. Contracts might last a week, two weeks or a month. Since school-age children also enjoy star charts, the contract could be part of a larger chart system, or vice versa. Checklists or charts provide immediate encouragement. The contract could list the number of points or stars required for a larger goal.

For children 5 and younger, the contract should last only one day. Keep contracts very simple, using only one behavior and one reward.

SAMPLE CONTRACT 2

CONTRACT BETWEEN: Mr. & Mrs. White   **AND**   Amanda

Effective Dates: May 7, 1999   **to**   June 7, 1999

In exchange for:

a ride to the movies on Saturday
night to meet her friends
(Amanda's parents will take her
to and from the movies)

Amanda   **agrees:**

to come home directly after school
activities during the week, and to
remain at home alone or with
girlfriends until her parents arrive.

In exchange for:

the privilege of staying overnight
once per week with a girlfriend

Amanda   **agrees:**

to babysit her younger brother on
Saturday mornings (without pay).

In exchange for:

a shopping trip to a nearby city
once per semester (money limit
agreed on in advance)

Amanda   **agrees:**

to participate in one of the
following extracurricular activities
(for the semester): band, theatre,
volleyball or ski club.

Date: _____   **Signed:** _____

(teen)

_____

(parents)

This contract will be reviewed   2   weeks from date of agreement, on   May 21, 1999

Behavioral Contracts

1. Use creative problem-solving to discuss and negotiate the contract.
2. Describe behavior and rewards specifically.
3. Suggest positive behaviors rather than listing what should be avoided.
4. Be sure the contract is fair.
5. Design the contract to be successful.
6. Follow basic positive reinforcement principles.
7. Phase out contracts when they no longer seem needed.

EXERCISES

Contracts

Practical Exercise

What's wrong with these contracts?

1. Corey's parents decided that if Corey, age 14, would do his homework every night for a month, they would take him to his favorite amusement park.

2. Andy, age 10, agreed to behave better in the evenings. Andy's parents agreed to take him to the movies on Friday night if he acted better that week. Andy likes going to the movies with his parents.

3. Overweight June, age 12, made a contract with her parents not to eat sweets. If she stayed away from sweets for two months, her parents would buy her the bicycle she had admired. June was good about skipping sweets at home, but often ate sweets at friends' homes.

Contracts

4. Misty's parents explained to Misty, age 16, that whenever she violated curfew, she couldn't go out on the next available evening.

5. David, age 8, agreed to try contracting with his parents. If he makes his bed every morning for a week, David's parents said he could stay overnight at Grandma's house on the weekend. David is not sure he likes the contract.

Write a contract between Jeremy and his parents.

Jeremy, age 10, absentmindedly lingers on his way to school in the morning. He is frequently late. His parents and his teacher have talked with him, he has stayed in for recess, but he still dawdles on his way to school. Jeremy loves airplanes and being around pilots. He wants to be a pilot when he is older. He likes to read magazines about flying and sometimes buys model planes.

Personal Exercise

1. Choose one of your child's behaviors that you would like to change by using a contract.

2. Describe the behavior so that it can be observed and measured (counted).

3. Choose a reward that will motivate the child to do well. Discuss this with your child.

4. Negotiate a contract with your child. Write the contract simply and clearly. Both parties sign. Is the contract concrete, specific, stated positively, fair, and designed to be successful?

5. Can your child receive reinforcement for the undesirable behavior from another source? (If yes, alter the contract or choose a different technique.)

6. Observe and measure the behavior for one week.

7. After one week, review the contract, Is it working? Could it be revised to be more effective? If so, how?

Time Out

Jonathan, age 4, and Stewart, age 2, liked to roughhouse, growing bolder as the game progressed. Eventually one of the boys would get hurt. Their mother tried "I messages," warnings and lectures, but nothing seemed to work.

Finally the boys' mother asked Jonathan and Stewart to sit in separate corners. She set a kitchen timer for two minutes and told them they could return to play when the bell rang.

Jonathan and Stewart's mother chose *time out* as a discipline technique. She used a boring time in the corner as a consequence for roughhousing. The "Law of the Soggy Potato Chip" described in chapter 8 explains that children would rather have negative attention than no attention at all. Time out uses this principle by offering no attention—a boring time—as a consequence to a child's behavior.

When time out is used to separate children who are fighting, it is considered a *logical consequence* (discussed in chapter 8), because being separated from your friend is related to the action of fighting. When time out is not related to the child's action, it is considered an *unrelated consequence* (discussed separately in this chapter). Time outs used for refusing to pick up toys, for not telling the truth, for jumping on the bed or for skipping chores are examples of unrelated consequences. Time outs used as logical consequences are more effective at teaching internal controls. (This is the reason logical consequences are located earlier on the discipline gradient.)

This section on time out is divided into two parts: (a) time out (the behaviorist view), and (b) time out variation.

Time out: behaviorist view

In the behaviorist view, time out equals boredom, which children would do anything to avoid.

■ How to use this technique

A time out is sending the child to a room (or part of a room) by herself as a consequence to her behavior. Time out interrupts unacceptable behavior by temporarily removing the child from the situation. After the child has been away from the scene for a short time, she is allowed to return. The rule for length of time outs is usually one minute per year of the child's age. A child who is four years old would spend four minutes in time out. A nine-year-old child would spend nine minutes in time out. (Time out is not effective with teens or with children under two years of age.)

Time out is effective because it is boring. It does not provide any attention or distraction. Children do not like boring. They much prefer stimulation, and even negative attention is better than no attention at all.

Choose a time-out place that is out of the way, one which does not have distractions. A hallway, a corner of the living room or a chair are good choices. Bedrooms are not the first choice for time-out locations for two reasons: bedrooms have too many distractions, and it is probably better not to correlate a child's bedroom with the less pleasant experience of time out. There are enough bedtime separation issues without associating time out and sleeping. For a similar reason, I recommend keeping time outs out of bathrooms—it is better not to connect unpleasantness with using the bathroom.

Explain time out to a child before you use it. Walk a young child through the steps the first few times. Tell her what time out is, when it occurs and exactly what happens.

The actual time out begins when crying and whining stops. (The exception might be with a toddler to whom you are teaching the concept.)

Time out should not turn into a time to complain or cry—the purpose is to provide a boring time for a child as a consequence to behavior.

Tell the child when time out is over. Many children respond well to the use of kitchen timers during time out. When the bell rings, the child may return to play. The timer helps distance the parent from the consequence, allowing the child to assume more of the responsibility for her own behavior. Children can even set the timer themselves.

Be consistent and matter-of-fact about using time out. Do not talk or argue with the child before or during a time out (except to tell her to take one). Talking or arguing with the child during the time out reinforces the child's undesirable behavior.

You may want to talk to your child about what happened. It is actually more helpful to discuss it at a different time—not when it has just occurred or is likely to occur. When you and your child are both calm (not upset from the discipline situation), your child is more likely to give you her complete attention. Lecturing the child after a time out is not helpful. Time out is not designed to help a child consider her actions—it is designed to provide a boring interlude which will deter her from repeating her action.

If the parent is able to catch the child in desirable behavior after a time out, this is an excellent time to reinforce the behavior. For example, Ricky receives a time out if he plays roughly with the cat. After the time out, Ricky's mother watches to see if he is petting the cat gently. As soon as Ricky pets gently, his mother gives him positive social reinforcement, such as, "That's great, Ricky. I like to see you playing gently with kitty."

■ Why is this technique valuable?

Time out is more effective than punishment, since punishment still offers negative attention which reinforces the undesirable behavior. Time out is a consequence when imposed calmly as a result of unacceptable behavior.

Time out interrupts the undesirable behavior immediately. It stops hitting, biting and other potentially dangerous behaviors, allowing time to pass and the child to calm down.

Time out can be used with more than one child at a time.

Time out, especially when used with choices or consequences, places the responsibility of the child's action on the child. It saves the parent from imposing judgments or punishments. When the child knows in advance that a certain action will bring a time out, the time out becomes a consequence of that behavior. For example, in the Greens' house where there are several small children, slamming doors brings an automatic time out. When a child slams a door, Mr. or Mrs. Green can lead that child to the time-out chair without saying a word. The child knows it is her own action that has led to sitting in the chair; the time out is not an angry reaction by a parent.

In the same way, *choices* (discussed in chapter 5) can be used with time outs to help teach responsibility for behavior. If a child is climbing on the furniture, the parent can state, "Stay off the furniture, or you will have a time out. *You choose.*" If the child continues to climb, the parent takes him to a time-out corner. In this case, the child has chosen the consequence that came with the action.

Time Out — Behaviorist View

1. Explain time out to the child before you use it.
2. Choose a time-out place that is free of distractions.
3. Send the child to the time-out place by herself as a consequence to her behavior.
4. Allow the child to return to the scene after a short time has passed (usually one minute per year of the child's age).
5. Do not consider crying or whining as part of the time-out period (except for very young or exceptional children).
6. Tell the child when time out is over, or provide a timer.
7. Do not talk or argue with the child before or during a time out.
8. Reinforce appropriate behavior following time out (do not lecture your child).

■ Cautions

Try not to use time outs for too many infractions. Time out is listed high on the gradient, which means it is not the best teacher of internal controls. Can other methods of discipline be used for a child's behavior? If so, try methods listed earlier on the gradient before using time out.

Time out should not be used as punishment that awards attention (see the "Law of the Soggy Potato Chip" in chapter 8). Time out becomes punishment when the parent is angry or scolds and lectures the child during the time out.

Time out should be *boring,* and should be administered in a calm, collected and prompt manner. When the time is up, announce "the time is up," or "the time out is over," (not "you can come out now"). Wording the phrase impersonally contributes to a matter-of-fact attitude.

If the child refuses to go to the time-out place, the parent should physically take him there and keep him there for the allotted time. During that time, the parent should offer as little attention as possible. For example, a toddler who will not stay in a time-out corner can be kept there by a parent who stands in front of him, but with his back to the toddler so as to offer minimum attention.

■ When to use this technique

Choose a few of the most important rules in your house (often safety issues) that will have automatic time outs. For example, hitting, biting, pushing and throwing things are automatic time outs in our house. Prepare children in advance—when the behavior occurs, they know that a time out is the consequence.

Use time outs at other times when there does not seem to be another discipline alternative.

Use time outs away from home when necessary. When shopping, visiting or doing other away-from-home activities, a time out in the car is usually quite successful. If your car is not available, try an adjoining room, a corner of a room or a hallway. When away from home, do not leave your child completely by himself in another room. Your child may be afraid if he cannot see you or know where you are during his time out.

■ Ages of children

Time out works best between ages 3 and 10. Time out rarely works with teens.

Time out can be greatly simplified for use with toddlers and older babies. Time out can be as simple as moving the child a short distance away from the situation. After the situation is under control, return to her and, after a very brief explanation, reinforce appropriate behavior. With children under three, keep the length of time out very short—even less than a minute when first starting out.

Modify time out as necessary with very young children. You might withdraw to another room for a short time, leaving the child behind. An older baby can be given a modified time out by putting her down and turning your back for a few minutes to show your disapproval of biting or pulling hair. A toddler can learn how to sit in a corner for a minute when he hits another child, even if you need to stand (with your back turned) nearby.

EXERCISES

Time Out

Practical Exercise

What is wrong with this time-out situation?

Crystal, five years old, was teasing her two-year-old brother Mark. Mother scolded, "Stop that, Crystal!" Crystal stopped teasing for a few minutes, but started again as soon as Mother's attention turned elsewhere.

"I told you to stop that, Crystal!" Mother was angry. She reached down and pulled Crystal to her feet. "Go stand in the corner and take a time out!"

"I don't wanna," whined Crystal, and slumped to the floor.

"You have to," snapped Mother. "Go right now."

"But how come Mark never gets yelled at?" whined Crystal.

"Because you always start it," said Mother. "Now go!" She pushed Crystal toward the corner.

Crystal reluctantly shuffled into the corner, still whining softly. Mark, who had been quiet until now, got to his feet and followed Crystal. Feeling protected, he darted into the corner and lightly slapped his sister on the arm.

"Mom!" protested Crystal. She started out of the corner toward her Mother.

"No, you have to stay there until I say you can come out. In 10 minutes."

Crystal continued to whine. Occasionally she muttered threats to her brother. Mark teased her for a short time but then began playing by himself. Mother returned to her work. Finally Crystal was quiet.

A few minutes later Mother called, "You can come out now, Crystal, if you can behave."

Crystal walked out of the corner still pouting. She avoided her brother, picked up a book and sat by herself to look at it. A few minutes later she started playing blocks with Mark while Mother was talking on the phone. But before Mother had finished her phone conversation, Crystal was teasing her brother again.

Personal Exercise

Should you use time out with your child?

1. Does your child understand the concepts of "wait" and "quiet"?

2. For what unacceptable behavior(s) would you use time out?

3. How long would time out be for your child?

4. What location would you choose for the time out? (It should be far enough away from activity so the child does not provoke attention, but close enough so she knows what she is missing.)

5. How would you explain time out to your child? (Use exact words.)

6. In what ways could you reinforce acceptable behavior after your child returned from a time out?

Time out variation

A *time out variation* is when the child chooses time away from a situation that may cause her to lose control. Although this can be called "time out," it is actually a much different situation than the time out discussed above. In this case, the child is encouraged to take time away from a situation which is about to become a problem. The child may choose to go to her room, or to another special corner filled with gentle activities—such as books and music—that will help her calm herself. Usually the child decides when she is ready to return to the original scene. This is a very positive strategy, especially for children who tend to lose control easily. The parent assists by providing the quiet corner, encouraging the child to take advantage of it when she is about to lose control, and positively reinforcing the child when she returns.

Jane Nelsen and H. Stephen Glenn, in *Time Out: Abuses and Effective Uses,* agree with this time out variation. Nelsen and Glenn caution that time out should not be made into a humiliating experience for the child—humiliation increases the child's discouragement and decreases his self-esteem. Nelsen and Glenn propose using time out as a time to cool off and feel better. They suggest allowing the child to decide how long he needs to stay in time out. By timing himself, the child is responsible for knowing when he is ready to come back out into activity.

■ How to use this technique

Choose a room or part of a room to be the location of the time out variation. You may call this location time out, or the sunshine corner, or the happy bench—a name which reflects the purpose of cooling down and gaining control before reentering activity. Decide whether to put quiet toys, books or music in the sunshine corner, according to your preference and knowledge of your child.

Explain to the child the purpose of this time out variation—which is to take some time to calm down when upset, and to come back into activity when ready.

When the child is involved in inappropriate behavior, such as hitting or pushing, *tell him that it appears he needs some cooling-off time,* or that his behavior suggests he needs some time to feel better. Ask him to go to the happy corner and stay there until he feels better and is ready to play cooperatively again.

Children should feel free to choose the time out variation by themselves if they feel they need time to control their feelings and actions.

■ Why is this technique valuable?

The advantages of this time out variation over the behaviorist version described first include greater emphasis on teaching internal controls and less strain on adult-child relationships. The time out variation would appear before the behaviorist version on the discipline gradient.

■ Cautions

If a child consistently chooses to spend time in the sunshine corner, the adult should consider why this is so. It may be a child's way of saying that something else is wrong. Most children prefer to be actively involved in the group. If a child uses the sunshine corner to withdraw from activities, that child may need special help.

■ When to use this technique

Use the time out variation whenever you would normally use a time out (behaviorist version).

■ Ages of children

The time out variation is particularly useful for preschool and school-age children. However, it also may work with preteens and teens, depending on the family. Toddlers can be introduced to the idea and helped to understand its function.

Time Out Variation

1. Explain time out to the child before you use it.
2. Provide a quiet corner or room filled with calming activities such as books and music.
3. Encourage the child to take time away from a situation which is about to become a problem and to use the activities in the time-out corner to calm herself.
4. Allow the child to decide when she is ready to return to the scene.
5. Do not talk or argue with the child before or during a time out.
6. Reinforce appropriate behavior following time out (do not lecture your child).

EXERCISES

Time Out Variation

Practical Exercise

Go back to the practical exercise on page 194 for the time-out example (behaviorist view).

How could Crystal and Mark's mother use the time out variation for this situation? Be sure to include Mark's role and Mother's response.

Personal Exercise

How would you use the time out variation in your home?

1. What location would you choose? What toys, books and other objects would be found there?

2. What would you call this location (e.g., time out, sunshine corner, the quiet place)?

3. Which of your child's behaviors would trigger time out?

4. How would you prepare your child in advance?

5. What would you say if your child was engaged in undesirable behavior and you wanted him to go to the quiet place?

6. How do you think your child would respond to using time out in this way?

Unrelated Consequences

When a child's action does not have an acceptable *natural conse-quence* and the parent cannot think of a *logical consequence* related to the child's action, the parent might impose an *unrelated consequence*.

For example, Jimmy left the bike out in the rain. Jimmy's parents are not willing to allow the bike to rust or be stolen (natural conse-quences). Nor do they want to lock the bike away for a few days (logi-cal consequences). They decide to ban Jimmy's television watching for one week.

Unrelated consequences help change behaviors. However, they are not very effective at teaching self-discipline, since controls are imposed on the child which are not related to the child's action.

This section is divided into three parts:
(a) unrelated consequences,
(b) *Grandma's rule* (also includes the *broken record*, an assertive dis-cipline technique that complements Grandma's rule), and
(c) grounding—some specific comments.

Unrelated consequences

Unrelated consequences are the same as logical consequences (cov-ered in chapter 8) except for two differences:
1. They are not related to the child's action, therefore they are actually easier to think up, since any consequence that is fair will work.
2. They are much less effective at teaching internal controls.

■ How to use this technique

To use an unrelated consequence, impose a fair, unrelated result to your child's undesirable behavior, such as assigning a chore or canceling play.

Examples of unrelated consequences:
When George got into a fight at school, Dad made him stay home all day Saturday, cleaning the house.

Ginny's telephone privileges were suspended for a week after she was caught lying to her mother.

David wasn't allowed to watch television because he was bossy and stubborn on the playground that afternoon.

Some consequences are either logical or unrelated depending on how they are used. Time out (discussed separately in this chapter) is a *logical consequence* when used to remove the child from a social situation when he hits another child. However, time out is frequently used as an unrelated consequence whenever the child does something the parent doesn't like. Time out is an *unrelated consequence,* for example, when used for slamming a door.

Grounding (discussed later in this section) can also be used as either a logical or an unrelated consequence. If a teen abuses her curfew or car privileges, she might be grounded for a time as a *logical consequence.* Grounding is an *unrelated consequence,* however, if used because a teen received poor grades at school.

■ Why is this technique valuable?

Unrelated consequences are not as useful as other techniques, because they rely heavily on external controls and thus are not good teachers of self-discipline. They also do not improve parent-child relationships. However, in the short run they produce behavioral change with minimal effort. Also, an unrelated consequence is more effective than shouting, threatening or spanking, since it does not offer negative attention as reinforcement.

■ Cautions

Don't get in the habit of using unrelated consequences as a frequent discipline technique. This technique is far to the right on the discipline gradient because it is clearly not a good teacher of internal controls. Use it in isolated instances, for serious offenses or in combination with other techniques that teach internal controls.

There is a fine line between unrelated consequences and punishment. *Punishment* is a penalty imposed for wrongdoing, with the idea of retribution rather than correction. Punishment is often accompanied by anger, and is frequently harsh or unreasonable (see chapter 10 for more about punishment).

To keep unrelated consequences from becoming punishment:
1. think things through in advance,
2. keep anger in control (or better yet, wait until the anger passes, then impose the consequence), and
3. be sure the consequence is not unreasonable for the offense.

▮ When to use this technique

Choose unrelated consequences if techniques farther to the left on the gradient do not work, and if there are no appropriate related consequences for a child's action.

Using prevention or communication techniques along with unrelated consequences helps teach internal controls and enhance relationships. For example, a parent might use an "I message" before imposing unrelated consequences.

▮ Ages of children

Unrelated consequences work with any age child. However, babies and toddlers—because of limited understanding—are less likely to understand or learn from unrelated consequences.

Unrelated Consequences

1. Use unrelated consequences in isolated instances for serious offenses.
2. Combine unrelated consequences with other techniques that are better at teaching internal controls.
3. Think through alternatives before imposing the consequence.
4. Choose a consequence that is not unreasonable for the offense.

EXERCISES

Unrelated Consequences

Practical Exercise

*Tell whether the following consequences are **logical** (related to the child's action) or **unrelated.***

1. The child won't eat his vegetables. The parent gives him a time out.

2. The child fights with his sister. The parent gives him a time out.

3. The child makes a big fuss about going to bed. The parent says that the child has used up storytime with her fussing, and will not get a bedtime story tonight.

4. The teen cheated on exams. His parents ground him for two weeks.

5. The teen comes home two hours late for weeknight curfew. The parents ground her for two weeks.

6. The teen is seen driving the car faster than the speed limit. The parents ground the teen for two weeks.

Suggest unrelated consequences for the following actions:

1. Your seven-year-old keeps forgetting to turn in his homework.

2. Your four-year-old teases her younger sister.

3. Your fourteen-year-old forgets to call you after school to tell you where he is.

Personal Exercise

1. Describe an undesirable action by your child that has not responded well to other discipline techniques.

2. Can you think of a logical consequence for this action? If yes, what is it? Are you willing to use the logical consequence for this action? Why or why not?

3. Whether your answer to #2 above is "yes" or "no," choose an unrelated consequence to your child's action.

4. Is your child old enough to understand why he/she received the unrelated consequence?

5. Is the consequence reasonable for the offense?

Grandma's rule and the broken record

Grandma's rule is the converse of unrelated consequences. Unrelated consequences are normally stated: If you do not do what I want you to do, then you may not do (or have) what you want. Grandma's rule is unrelated consequences in reverse: *Do first what I want you to do, then you may do what you want to do.*

Described by Wesley Becker in *Parents Are Teachers*, Grandma's rule tells parents to require the work first, then allow the play. For example, if the child wants to go out to play, make sure the chores are done first. If the child wants a snack and she has been procrastinating about picking up her toys, require the cleanup before she can have the snack.

The work required first by Grandma's rule does not have to be related (or unrelated) to the play that follows, although related consequences are better at teaching internal controls.

■ How to use this technique

To use Grandma's rule, *clearly state that your request must be done before the behavior the child desires. Then back it up with the broken record* (explained below).

Examples of Grandma's rule:
You may watch television after your toys are all put away.

You may go out to play after you finish your homework.

We will read a story together after you do your chores.

Grandma's rule is common sense. However, children often respond to Grandma's rule in predictable ways. Barbara Coloroso, in *Kids Are Worth It,* describes the *three cons:*
1. *Pleading and promising:* "Oh *please,* Mom. Just this *one* time. I *promise* I'll do my homework as soon as I return from the playground."
2. *Comparisons and anger:* "Everyone *else* gets to go to the playground after school. No one *else* has to stay home and do their homework first. Everyone else does it after dinner. Why do *I* have to do it now?" and "You're mean! I hate you!" (slams door).
3. *Resistance and sulking:* "Make me. I won't do it."
Coloroso suggests using the *broken record,* a technique that comes from the field of assertiveness training. The broken record is saying the statement over and over again—like a broken record—in response to any or all of the cons.

Example of the broken record:

Linda runs in the front door after school and drops her books on the table. "Hi Mom. I'm going to the playground with Colleen and Mandy."

Mom replies, "You must do your homework first before you go to the playground." *(Grandma's rule)*

"I know, Mom, but they're going to practice softball today, and I want to play."

"You may go to the playground after you do your homework." *(restatement of Grandma's rule)*

"Please, Mom. I want to play softball today. I promise I'll do my homework as soon as I return." *(Con 1)*

"You may go to the playground after you do your homework." *(broken record)*

"Aw, Mom. Just for today. They're practicing and I don't want to miss it. I won't forget my homework." *(more Con 1)*

"You may go to the playground after you do your homework." *(broken record)*

"None of the other kids have to do their homework first. The other moms wouldn't make their kids miss softball! Why do *I* have to miss it!" *(Con 2)*

"You may go to the playground after you do your homework." *(broken record)*

"Oh, come on, Mom, I already told you I'd do my homework as soon as I return!" *(Con 1)*

"You may go to the playground after you do your homework." *(broken record)*

"Mom! Why do you keep saying that! You're mean! I wish you weren't my mother!" *(Con 2)*

"You may go to the playground after you do your homework." *(broken record)*

"Oh, okay! I'll do my homework!" Linda grabs her books and runs upstairs to her room.

If Linda's mother were to give in to Linda during any of the cons, she would actually be reinforcing them, and Linda would be learning to manipulate her mother. By using the broken record technique, Linda's mother distances herself from Linda's comments, and thus is not swayed or hurt by them. But more importantly, she sets the stage for future encounters. Linda will learn that conning doesn't work with her mother.

Many children, like Linda, don't even reach the third con before the situation is resolved. However, some children seem to prefer Con 3, even starting out with it.

For example:

Kurt, age 6, comes to the dinner table and finds no place set for him.

"Where's my plate?"

"You may eat as soon as you pick up your toys."

"No, I don't wanna!"

"You may eat as soon as you pick up your toys."

"Okay. I won't eat."

"You may eat as soon as you pick up your toys."

"I won't eat. You can't make me pick them up." Kurt leaves, going into his bedroom and slamming the door.

Ten minutes later Kurt returns and sits down at the table. "They're picked up. Can I have my dinner now?"

■ Why is this technique valuable?

Grandma's rule and the broken record, like unrelated consequences, rely heavily on external controls. But in the short run they produce behavioral change with minimal effort. In addition, the broken record helps parents to be consistent, and consistency stops needless repetition of the same problems. Grandma's rule and the broken record discourage children from manipulating parents to get their own way.

■ Cautions

When using Grandma's rule, *don't allow the child to do what he wishes by accepting his promise that the work will be done later.* The main incentive of Grandma's rule is that the work must be done first. The play becomes a reward for doing the work.

When children use one or more of the three cons, don't let your emotions be swayed by their reasoning. Be aware of con logic and stick to the broken record. In this way, the children will learn to carry out their responsibilities first, and will also begin to use the cons less and less as they discover that conning doesn't work.

■ When to use this technique

Choose Grandma's rule and the broken record if other techniques farther down on the gradient do not work, and if you cannot think of related consequences for a child's action.

Using prevention or communication techniques along with Grandma's rule and the broken record will help teach internal controls and enhance relationships.

■ Ages of children

Use Grandma's rule and the broken record with preschoolers, school-age children and teens.

Toddlers may also respond to Grandma's rule and the broken record. However, because toddlers are working on independence issues, you may find yourself in an impasse with a toddler when using these techniques. It may be simpler and less stressful for all to just pick up your toddler and take him where he needs to go. Don't give in partway when you use Grandma's rule and the broken record with toddlers, because giving in even once will teach them that they can outlast you to get their way.

Grandma's Rule

Do first what I want you to do, then you may do what you want to do.

The Broken Record

Calmly say your statement over and over again—like a broken record—in response to a child's protests. ("You may go to the playground after you do your homework.")

EXERCISES

Grandma's Rule and the Broken Record

Practical Exercise

Use Grandma's rule for the following situations. What would you say to the child?

1. Mary Ann did not make her bed this morning. She is watching television before dinner.

2. Dan wants to go outside and ride his bike. He did not do his daily chores yet.

3. Timmy, who is potty-training, would like a cookie as a snack. He has not used the potty all morning.

What con is each child using below? What should the parent say next in this exchange, if the parent is using the broken record?

4. Parent: "You may go to the party after you take your brother to his piano lesson."
   Child: "You always make me take him everywhere! You're mean and unfair!"
   What con is she using? _____ What should the parent say?

5. Parent: "I'll read you a story as soon as you put on your pajamas."
   Child: "Debbie never has to put on her pajamas so early. Why do I have to?"
   What con is he using? _____ What should the parent say?

6. Parent: "You may have dessert as soon as you have finished your dinner."
   Child: "But I ate all my potatoes, and most of my peas."
   What con is she using? _____ What should the parent say?

7. Parent: "We will go to the store as soon as you pick up your toys."
   Child: "I'll pick them up as soon as we get back, I promise."
   What con is he using? _____ What should the parent say?

8. Parent: "Your friend can come over as soon as you change your clothes."
   Child: "I won't change my clothes. You can't make me."
   What con is he using? _____ What should the parent say?

9. Parent: "You may go to the library after this week's chores are finished."
   Child: "Mom! No one else has that yucky rule. Why do I have to finish them first? Jackie and Lynn don't even have weekly chores!"
   What con is she using? _____ What should the parent say?

Personal Exercise

1. Describe a situation with your child where you would like to be firm without giving in.

2. What things does your child say that make you give in? For each statement, which con is he/she using?

3. Choose a "Grandma's rule" statement for the situation you described in #1.

4. Write out a likely conversation with your child about the above situation, using the broken record and labeling cons if you can.

Grounding

"You're grounded for two months!"

What does it mean? She can't leave the house for two months? She can't leave the house for two months, except for school? How about church? Driving her brother to piano lessons? Going over to a friend's house to study for exams? Talking on the telephone?

Two months! Will mom and dad be able to last with a teen full time in the house, without even telephone privileges, for two months?

Grounding (or restriction) means different things to different families. For some families, all social privileges are suspended and the child must stay at home except for school or church activities. For other families, there are different levels of grounding:

1. loss of weekend social activities with friends
2. loss of weekend plus weeknight out-of-home social activities with friends
3. loss of 1 and 2 above plus loss of weeknight in-home activities with friends
4. 1, 2 and 3 above plus loss of weekend phone privileges
5. 1 through 4 above plus loss of all phone privileges
6. 1 through 5 above plus loss of weekend shared family outings
7. 1 through 6 above plus loss of weekly shared family outings.

Grounding is considered a *logical consequence* if the child's action is related in some way, such as in the case of a child who doesn't call home after school to tell his family where he is. Often grounding is used as an *unrelated consequence*—because grades were poor, or a fight occurred at school, or the child is caught in a lie.

The technique of grounding uses external controls.

■ How to use this technique

Decide what offenses will have grounding as a consequence. *Choose serious offenses that have not been resolved through other techniques* such as logical consequences or contracts. Grounding will work more effectively if it is related to the child's action, and if it is used sparingly.

Decide what level of grounding (see breakdown on the previous page) *is useful to act as a consequence without producing undue resentment or rebellion.* Remember that you have to live with the grounded teen. Does she really have to skip shared family activities? If your teen is grounded, she may appreciate fun time with the family, and her parents may appreciate the chance to be together and work on rebuilding relationships.

Similarly, does grounding mean you have to restrict the phone? Teens have a very strong need to be in touch with their peers. The phone can be a healthy outlet, even while the teen is on restriction. *Allowing phone use can minimize resentment and provide relief for both teen and parent.* One parent said she never restricted phone privileges for her grounded teen, because when her daughter commiserated by phone with her friends, she frequently found out that the friend had more severe restrictions!

Decide what length of time grounding will cover. *Choose a time acceptable to you, the parent, as well as a time which is reasonable for the child.* Two months is a *very* long time to have a sulky teen restricted to the house.

Don't feel trapped into making a grounding decision on the spur of the moment. Tell your child you need some time to decide how long and what restrictions will occur. Even if you told her yesterday that she is grounded until spring, it's all right to change your mind the next morning in favor of a more rational decision.

■ Why is this technique valuable?

A teen's freedom to interact with her peers is usually very important to her. Restricting that freedom is a strong consequence and will influence behavior.

■ Cautions

Don't use grounding for smaller offenses that can be resolved in other ways with techniques that are better at building internal controls. Use grounding only when the seriousness of the situation warrants it.

Don't take away too many freedoms at once. Total restriction is an awesome event for a teen. Don't require total restriction for less than an earthshaking event (and perhaps not even then). Consider taking away one privilege for one infraction.

Don't ground a teen for too long a time. You, as well as your teen, will have to live with the consequences of restriction. After several weeks have passed, it is tempting to shorten the sentence. Teens remember when we don't follow through on what we say.

■ When to use this technique

Use grounding when a serious behavior cannot be modified in other ways (such as logical consequences, problem-solving or contracts).

Use grounding when it is related to the child's actions (if possible). Grounding is more effective when used as a logical consequence.

Examples of related actions might be:
* Not coming directly home after school (school-age child), not phoning parent to say where she is,
* violating curfew,
* lying about whereabouts when out with friends,
* getting into trouble when out with friends (such as drinking or stealing).

■ Ages of children

Use grounding for teens.

Sometimes limited, simplified grounding or restriction is appropriate for school-age children, especially if it relates to the child's actions.

Grounding

1. Use grounding sparingly and only for serious offenses.
2. If possible, use grounding as a consequence related to the child's action.
3. Don't take away too many freedoms at once.
4. Don't ground a teen for too long a time.
5. Feel free to tell your child you need some time to decide how long and what restrictions will occur.
6. Combine grounding with other techniques that are better at teaching internal controls.

EXERCISES

Grounding

Practical Exercise

What type of grounding restrictions (if any) would you impose in the following situations?

1. Carrie, age 16, lied about going to her friend Mary's house for a slumber party. Carrie told her mother that it was only for girls and that Mary's mother would be home. Carrie's mother found out from another parent that it was a mixed group and that Mary's parents were away that weekend.

2. Margaret, age 11, comes home alone after school at 4:30 p.m. She is to remain at home until her mother arrives at 5:30 p.m. Margaret can visit girlfriends' homes if she calls her mother to tell her where she is. Last week Margaret and a girlfriend visited a boy's home after school, with no parent present. Margaret "forgot" to call her mother that day.

3. David, age 17, came home one hour late for midnight curfew Friday night. He did not call to say where he was.

4. Sheila, age 12, cheated on a geometry test.

5. Bob's parents found a six-pack of beer in the trunk of their car after Bob, age 16, used the car last Saturday night.

Personal Exercise

1. For what behaviors would you consider grounding your child? (If your child is not yet old enough, think ahead to the future.)

2. Choose one of the behaviors you listed in #1 above. Could you resolve this behavior by using another discipline technique? (If so, which?)

3. What level of grounding would you choose for the behavior listed in #2? (See the seven levels listed at the beginning of this section, or make up your own.)

4. For how long would you ground your child for the behavior listed in #2?

5. What do you think your child's reaction would be to the length and type of grounding that you chose in this exercise?

6. Would you ever consider total restriction (total suspension of freedoms) for any behavior of your child? If so, what behavior(s)? If not, why not?

Grounding

Chapter 10

The Difference Between Discipline and Punishment

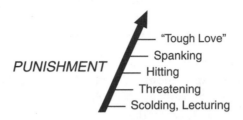

PUNISHMENT

— "Tough Love"
— Spanking
— Hitting
— Threatening
— Scolding, Lecturing

At the extreme end of the gradient are punishment techniques, which include scolding, lecturing, threatening, hitting, spanking and "Tough Love" (a technique for rebellious teens). Although the punishment techniques are briefly discussed in this chapter, much of the discussion centers on punishment as a whole, for two important reasons:

1. Nearly any response by a parent can be considered punishment if it includes anger on the part of the parent, unreasonableness or unfairness in the amount or type of consequence, and powerlessness on the part of the child.

2. Punishment is not as effective as other discipline techniques, because:

(a) It doesn't teach internal controls (self-discipline), but rather fosters hostility, resentment and powerlessness.
(b) Punishment still offers negative attention as a reinforcer.
(c) It loses power as the child grows older.
(d) It is often administered when the parent is angry and least in control.

What is punishment?

In the context of the discipline gradient, punishment is an unrelated consequence imposed on the child which is unreasonable or unfair, and which is accompanied by the parent's anger. When we are angry, it is easy to react to a child's inappropriate behavior by lashing out. We scold, or lecture, or shout or spank. Sometimes we use other techniques on the gradient, but with consequences that are unreasonable or administered with parental anger.

Examples:

Four-year-old Sarah hit her two-year-old brother in an argument. Sarah's mother scolded her angrily, ordered her into a ten-minute time out, and lectured her several times after the time out was over, calling her a "bad girl who didn't care about others."

Twelve-year-old Jason visited a girlfriend's house (her mother was present) after school without telling his parents. When confronted with the evidence, he lied about it. His parents lectured him angrily for an hour, then grounded him for the rest of the semester (two and a half months) with no privileges.

In each of the above cases, the parents used punishment to respond to their child's behavior, even though both time out and grounding are not found in the punishment section of the gradient. What transformed these two behavior management techniques into punishment were:

1. anger on the part of the parent, which tends to frighten and devalue the child (see more about anger in chapter 11);
2. unreasonable consequences (Sarah's time out should have been three minutes, not ten minutes; Jason's grounding time was too long for his infraction);
3. powerlessness on the part of the child—in both cases, the punishment was imposed on the child without any discussion or input by the child.

Punishment techniques frequently include physical or psychological hurt.

Scolding and lecturing often focus on the "you" discussed in chapter 6 in the section about "I messages." "You always come home late." "You never clean up after yourself." "Why can't you be considerate of others?" "You messages" destroy self-esteem, reinforcing feelings of worthlessness.

Threatening is telling our children we are going to do something to them (usually unpleasant), but then not carrying it out. Children quickly learn that threats have no follow-through. Besides being ineffective, threats weaken the child's trust in the parent.

Hitting (such as slapping a child's fingers) has the same disadvantages as spanking.

Spanking models aggressive behavior, as well as providing dangerous opportunities for hurting children. Some child psychologists say that parents should never spank their children—the potential for physical pain and the strain on parent-child relationships just isn't worth it. Other psychologists say that we are only human; sometimes a quick spank (parent's hand on the child's bottom) is a way to clear the air and start over together. (There is widespread agreement that anything stronger than a parent's hand on a child's bottom is too much. Causing physical pain for the purposes of control is not effective in the long run, and is abusive.)

It is the parents' decision whether to use spanking or not. But parents who will have the most problems regarding spanking are the parents who are using it for every small infraction. If a child is spanked for not sharing a toy, for running in the grocery store, for talking back to her mother or for throwing food on the floor, what options remain when she hits the baby, steals or plays with matches? If a parent starts with a technique at the very end of the gradient (spanking), there is nowhere to go for new responses to stronger behaviors.

When deciding whether or not to spank your child, consider the four disadvantages to punishment discussed below.

Four strong disadvantages to punishment

1. Punishment doesn't teach internal controls (self-discipline), but rather fosters hostility, resentment and powerlessness. When an unfair consequence is angrily imposed on a child, the chances of learning from that situation are very small. Instead the child tends to feel resentful, defensive and powerless.

Think of a situation where another adult tried to angrily impose her will on you. Perhaps it was a boss who scolded, lectured or fired you. Or a spouse or an ex-spouse who tried to lay anger, blame and guilt on your shoulders. Or how about the mortgage company who was ready to repossess your car without giving you a reasonable hearing? In the presence of anger, blame or unreasonable consequences, we become defensive, angry and resentful. It isn't fair. If we've made a mistake, we should be able to atone for it and go on from there.

Hitting a child does not teach a child to stop hitting. The original frustration which caused the child's action coupled with the unfairness of the response (actual or perceived) causes resentment and hostility. In addition, if the child has no input into the consequence, a sense of powerlessness prevails, which leads to a pervasive feeling of "it's all their fault." The child does not accept responsibility for her actions, but rather blames the unfairness of others for consequences that result.

2. *Punishment is not as effective as other discipline techniques because it still offers negative attention as a reinforcer.* In the chapters on behavior management, we saw that parents reinforce negative behavior by offering negative attention when the child is behaving inappropriately. This is the "Law of the Soggy Potato Chip" (see chapter 8), stating that children will accept negative parental attention rather than receive no attention at all. Even though a spanking or a scolding is unpleasant, a child who is hungry for attention will willingly accept punishment rather than be ignored.

Also, after a punishment, the parent—who often feels guilty—tends to treat her child gently, to offer more positive attention than before the punishment. A child may not realize it consciously, but nonetheless becomes aware on a subtle level that after punishment comes a pleasant closeness. To the child, experiencing this closeness may be worth being punished.

3. *Punishment loses power as the child grows older.* Children are growing taller and reaching puberty at younger ages. When they outgrow our ability to spank them, what will we do then?

Children who are strictly taught by authoritarian parents to obey will learn obedience without questioning. When they become adolescents, they begin—as adolescents do—to shift more attention and allegiance to their peers. Having been taught to obey, these adolescents will continue to obey, but now they have a new center of authority—their peers. These teens will have a difficult time declining anything their peer group asks them to do.

The way to raise adolescents who are able to say no to drinking, drugs and premarital sex is to teach self-discipline through prevention and communication techniques (and behavior management techniques for the tougher problems). It takes longer in the beginning to use prevention and communication techniques to change behaviors. More time and effort are needed to sit down with children and teach creative problem-solving, to offer choices or to follow through on consequences that are related to children's behavior.

But if a parent is willing to invest time and effort on the non-punishment techniques on the gradient, that investment comes back with great reward. Children begin to solve their own problems. Bickering between siblings lessens. Grumbling diminishes; children begin to take responsibility for their actions. Self-esteem is high, and parents can feel more confident about their children facing the scary choices of adolescence.

Spanking may work in the short term—it may stop a child's action immediately. But reliance on spanking and other punishment will not build the skills your child needs to survive and thrive during adolescence.

4. Punishment is often administered when the parent is angry and least in control. Anger terrifies a child, causes him to internalize negative self-worth ("How bad I am to have caused this awful anger"), and also teaches negative anger responses through modeling. When we are angry, we are not thinking logically. We are more likely to lash out; we are less likely to care about our children's self-esteem. Because logic flees during anger, many parents tend to revert back to punishment techniques that were used in their own childhood years. (See chapter 11 for an in-depth discussion on anger.)

Although included on the discipline gradient, punishment is not equivalent to discipline. Discipline aims to teach internal controls; punishment aims to control behavior. Children often get the idea that being punished means you are a bad person.

The Difference Between Punishment and Discipline

PUNISHMENT	DISCIPLINE
comes from anger and/or stress	comes from desire to teach child
generally uses force	is based on mutual trust and respect, rather than force
is irrational; can't be defended	is based on appropriate expectations
is an unrelated consequence	is a related consequence
teaches what *not* to do	teaches what to do
lowers self-esteem of both parent & child	raises self-esteem of both parent & child
embarrasses child	helps child take responsibility
builds resentment	builds mutual respect
encourages lying, tattling, cheating, aggression	encourages communication; builds positive relationships

"Tough Love": On the discipline gradient, *Tough Love* refers to the parent support group that helps parents deal with rebellious teens or teens battling difficult problems such as drug use. Discussion of this problem area is beyond the scope of this book, but Tough Love support groups can be contacted directly in many cities. The reason for placing this technique at the very end of the discipline gradient is that part of the Tough Love program consists of a dramatic, last-resort process: if the teen does not follow the rules in the house, the teen is no longer welcome to live there. This technique is usually used only in extreme situations, when the teen is unwilling to change habits—such as drug use—that are disrupting the entire family. However, since it is such a drastic method, it is important to carefully explore all other possibilities, including family and teen counseling, before considering its use.

Punishment is not as effective as other discipline techniques, because:

1. It doesn't teach internal controls (self-discipline), but rather fosters hostility, resentment and powerlessness.
2. It offers negative attention as a reinforcer.
3. It loses power as the child grows older.
4. It is often administered when the parent is angry and least in control.

EXERCISES

Punishment

Practical Exercise

What makes each of the parent's reactions in the following situations punishment? What is a more effective way to handle each situation? (Try changing the punishment techniques in the following scenes into prevention, communication or behavior management techniques.)

1. Amanda, age 3, turned on the family computer without asking, and (by experimenting) erased three of her father's important business files. Amanda's mother scolded her at length, made her stay in her room for the rest of the afternoon, and promised that "she was really going to get a good whoppin' when her dad came home."

   Why are the parent's actions considered punishment?

   What is a more effective way to handle this situation?

2. David, age 2, threw a tantrum in the grocery store because he was tired and wanted to go home. His mother scolded and spanked him and made him walk beside the cart until they were finished shopping.
   Why are the parent's actions considered punishment?

   What is a more effective way to handle this situation?

3. Shawna, age 8, took a necklace from her friend's house without asking. Shawna received a spanking and was not allowed to go over to any friend's house for the next month.
   Why are the parent's actions considered punishment?

   What is a more effective way to handle this situation?

4. Candra, age 13, refused to do her weekly chores (cleaning the bathrooms and vacuuming). Dad slapped her across the face and told her not to "sass back."
   Why are the parent's actions considered punishment?

   What is a more effective way to handle this situation?

5. Joel, age 16, skipped gym class to go to the mall with his friend. Joel's parents (who found out from the friend's mother) confronted Joel angrily and told him he was completely grounded (no privileges) for two months.
   Why are the parent's actions considered punishment?

   What is a more effective way to handle this situation?

Personal Exercise

1. Describe a situation with your child where you use (or are tempted to use) punishment:
    child's behavior:

    your reaction:

    child's response:

    your reaction:

2. How do you think your child feels when he does this behavior?

3. How do you think your child feels after he has been punished for this behavior?

4. How do you feel when your child does this behavior?

5. How do you feel after you have punished your child?

6. What other techniques could you use with this behavior? Choose at least one technique from each of the following categories: prevention, communication and behavior management.

Chapter 11

Dealing with Anger and Stress

Anger and stress are combined in the same chapter because they often go together. Parenting is not an easy job. What other job asks a minimum of eighteen years' commitment, no pay and no vacations? In addition, the increase of stress has kept pace with the growth of technology and global access. Our human bodies still react with the same "fight or flight" physical response when we are stressed or angry: adrenaline floods the system, unneeded digestive and elimination processes are temporarily suspended, extra sugar is released by the liver and shunted to the muscles, and we feel as if we are about to explode. Our bodies are ready to fight or flee from the enemy. But the stresses of today's world have changed from the stresses of past societies, and the fight or flight response is no longer always the best way to react.

The advantage of the fight or flight response is the ability to meet great energy demands required in certain situations, such as the ability to fight or run from an attacker, or to save oneself or another in an emergency. The disadvantage of this physical condition is that sometimes no physical response is required when a person is under stress. The body is left with an overflow of energy it cannot use. For example, when a car narrowly misses a man as he crosses the street, he resumes his journey on the sidewalk, but his heart is still pounding, his breath is coming quickly and his nerves are still on edge. It takes quite a while for the adrenaline to leave the body and for the man to feel normal again.

Dealing with Anger

The anger response is physically similar to the flight or fight response of the body that is triggered when we are under great stress. However, the physical feelings of energy and explosiveness caused by anger usually don't help the situation. Many people release that explosiveness in a destructive manner.

Should anger be expressed, and if so, how?

There is a school of thought (especially prevalent in the 1960s and 1970s, but still around today) which says that it is healthy to express anger, and that it will fester and grow inside us if we do not express it. However, recent studies have shown that strong expression of anger tends to encourage the growth of more anger and of aggression. In her book *Anger: The Misunderstood Emotion,* Carol Tavris cites numerous studies that indicate strongly expressed anger breeds greater anger. Tavris says that experiencing catharsis and relief from expressing anger is a myth. Fired factory workers who were encouraged to brood about management tested higher in anger and resentment than those fired workers who were asked neutral questions. Students who were less quick to express anger were found to be more tolerant and flexible than students who expressed anger easily.

Part of the problem is that people are not rational when angry. Once anger has begun, it propels the person quickly toward the physical anger response which cries for expression. During this time the angry person is not thinking clearly. Anger twists and distorts perception.

An effective way to handle the irrationality and explosiveness of the anger response is to choose a constructive way to express anger, and to work on resolutions *after* the anger has dissolved. Otherwise the anger itself gets in the way of positive solutions, and causes hurt instead. This is illustrated in the "cycle of anger" diagram on the next page, created by Barbara Naki of Honolulu, Hawaii. The process of anger is shown as a cycle, beginning with unmet expectations and (moving counterclockwise) ending with a resolution to the problem.

Anger begins with unmet expectations. Expectations are often unmet because we haven't communicated them. For example, we might expect that a ten-year-old child (using common sense) would close the screen door behind him to keep out the mosquitoes. Or we might expect a three-year-old child to share his toys. But if we haven't told our children what we would like them to do, they are less likely to do it.

Even when we do communicate our expectations, sometimes they are not realistic. A ten-year-old boy, excited from the school field trip or tired after a long day, may very well forget the relationship between screen doors and mosquito bites. A three-year-old child, although old enough to know that sharing is required, is still young enough—and egocentric enough—to have a hard time parting with his possessions. Another example of an unrealistic expectation might be expecting a colicky baby to sleep through the night (or even for four hours straight).

Cycle of Anger

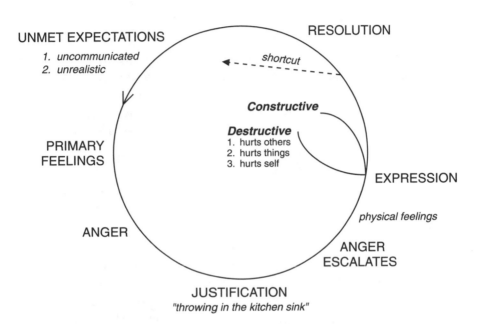

When expectations are unmet, first we feel disappointed, frustrated, unappreciated or any number of other emotions, depending on the situation. These feelings lead to anger. *Anger is a secondary emotion.* Other feelings (called *primary feelings* in the anger diagram) come first.

Anger is also an uncomfortable emotion. It doesn't feel good. So we tend to justify our feelings of anger by thinking of similar situations that have made us angry. Not only has my son invited in several mosquitoes by leaving the door open this afternoon, but he also left it open this morning, and yesterday and the day before. And he didn't make his bed this morning, and he left his clothes lying on the floor.... We start to "throw in the kitchen sink," anything else we can think of from the past that has frustrated us and has not been dealt with sufficiently.

The colicky baby is not only waking me up at three o'clock in the morning, but she didn't fall asleep until midnight! And last night was no better, and the night before...

By throwing in the kitchen sink, we justify our anger, which gives us an excuse to be angry. Unfortunately, having more to be angry about increases the amount of our anger. Pressure builds up; we begin to experience the physical characteristics of the anger response. The increased adrenaline and other physical changes pressure us for release. Some people feel hot and sweaty when they are angry; their faces might turn red. Others feel tightness in their stomachs, or find their fists or jaws clenched tightly. Some people shake when they are angry, or feel cold. Whatever the physical sensations, these are warnings that we are about to explode.

The explosion itself is called the expression of anger in the "Cycle of Anger" diagram. Anger can be expressed in constructive or destructive ways. Destructive expression of anger hurts one or more of the following: other people, things or ourselves.

Destructive anger can hurt others physically (through physical punishment or violence) and verbally. We tend to say the most hurtful comments when we are angry. "Why can't you ever learn..." "How many times have I told you..." "You'll never be a responsible person..." "I hate you...." We can apologize for our words, but we cannot erase them. Anger is not an acceptable excuse for hurting someone.

Destructive anger destroys physical items when people smash, throw, hit and tear things around them. Not only is there a physical loss, but children who watch their parents smash things in anger are learning through modeling that it is all right to smash when you are angry.

Destructive anger hurts ourselves when we turn the anger inward, either by physically hurting our self or our possessions, or by trying to submerge anger through unhealthy responses such as overeating, smoking, drinking or use of drugs. Getting in the car and driving when we are angry—and therefore irrational—puts all three (others, things and ourselves) in jeopardy.

On the other hand, it is possible to release the pent-up physical pressure of anger in constructive ways. Constructive methods of expressing anger include (a) activities that give a person time to calm down, letting excess adrenaline dissipate and allowing the body's cycles to return to normal, and (b) activities that allow the person to burn up the excess adrenaline in constructive ways. It is best to choose a constructive method of releasing anger *before* a person becomes angry, because *anger is irrational.* We are not thinking clearly when we are angry, and it is too difficult to stop in the middle of the anger response to choose a non-hurtful method of expression. In the chart below are some examples of constructive release of anger.

Constructive Ways to Release Anger

activities that allow adrenaline to dissipate	activities that burn off adrenaline
take a walk	clean the house
write in a journal	play a musical instrument
read	go for a bike ride
work on a hobby	exercise
listen to music	stack firewood
spend time alone	have a good cry

The best time to work on resolutions is after the anger is gone. When my husband and I were first married, I felt that we should work out problems while we were still angry, and not let the situation pass. I wanted to discuss the situation immediately, while I was focused on it. My husband's reaction to a quarrel, however, was to leave. (This disturbed me considerably!)

Discussing a problem while the parties are still angry has a strong disadvantage: angry people are irrational, and the discussion quickly escalates into a hurtful, nonproductive exchange. My husband's reaction was better than mine, in that he knew he was too angry to communicate. However, we eventually realized that he needed to let me know when he *would* be able to talk about it. Walking away from an argument without resolving it—without planning to talk about it later—causes a shortcut back to the original problem (see dotted line in the diagram) and another trip around the anger cycle, this time with more "kitchen sink" to throw in.

The key to resolving a situation is to *wait until the anger is gone and then problem-solve.* After the anger has dissipated, logical thinking returns and problem-solving skills start working again. The opportunities for hurt have passed. All of the techniques on the gradient—with the exception of punishment techniques, which are connected to anger—are possible solutions for effectively resolving the anger cycle. Sometimes solutions (especially those for unrealistic unmet expectations) require outside help. The parent with the colicky baby may need to find relatives and friends who can care for the baby for short periods of time, so the parent can take naps. The parent with the mosquito problem might install a spring on the screen door so that it closes automatically.

A common temptation is to swallow back the anger and "let it go this time." The danger to this is the shortcut back to the beginning of the anger cycle. If we do not resolve a problem, however small, it tends to slide into a backpack of unresolved issues that we carry around with us. Each time we do not resolve a situation, our backpack gets a little heavier. One day the backpack is overloaded, and we dump it all out on top of the person we are angry at. Trying to resolve a whole backpack of issues is almost impossible without the help of a trained counselor (and sometimes not even then). It is much better to resolve each issue as it occurs. But remember to wait until after the anger has passed. (If anger is so intense that it never dissipates, this is a strong sign that a counselor is needed.)

It is possible for some people to stop the cycle of anger by tuning in to their primary emotions—the feelings that come before anger. If a person is able to recognize the hurt, disappointment or frustration that leads to anger, she can deal with the primary feeling—moving into the resolution and skipping the whole irrational buildup, escalation and expression of anger. Ideally, this is how we would deal with our children's misbehaviors. For example, the parent might recognize the frustration she feels when she sees the screen door open, and might express this to her son using an "I message," instead of screaming at him in anger.

Practically speaking, however, it is very difficult to tune in to those subtle primary feelings. Anger has such a strong flavor that it tends to mask the other feelings around it. (Anger also occurs more frequently when we have built up a backpack of unresolved issues.) Most of us will be pulled into the irrational cycle of anger at one time or another. Some of us—influenced by hereditary or environmental differences—will have a harder time than others. But in each case, anger can be managed by expressing it constructively and resolving the issue after anger has dissolved.

Children also go through the anger cycle, but they tend to zip through it much faster than adults. They move very quickly from an unmet expectation to the expression of their anger. Children of any age can be shown constructive ways to express anger. What is acceptable in your home? Are children allowed to slam doors? The answer will differ, depending on the rules and needs of the people in your home. There are toys made that young children might use to express their anger, such as the wooden hammer-and-peg set, which has pegs set in holes on a rack which can be turned over and hammered again. Music, drama, puppets and visual arts are very effective ways to help children express anger. Angry puppets might punch pillows. Paper, crayons, paint and clay are effective tools to describe how a child feels. After the picture is drawn, a sensitive "tell me about it" can help the child express feelings verbally.

Another way to help children deal with their own anger is to provide a space where they can go to let the adrenaline settle down, a place to stay until they feel in control again. One family created a "sunshine corner" with a throw rug, soft music on cassettes with headsets, books and art materials. Their children (especially one child who had a particularly hard time with frustration) could go to the sunshine corner, listen quietly to music and read or draw, knowing that no one would interrupt them until they were ready to join the family again. And no one would tease them for needing a healthy time out.

If a child is old enough to cognitively understand the cycle of anger, show it to her, explain it, talk about it. Children—as well as many adults—are frightened by the way anger takes over and the potential for hurt. A group of angry preteens who learned about the cycle of anger were relieved to understand the irrationality of their anger, and to learn ways to control it. When children are not angry, talk about constructive ways to express anger; perhaps even practice some of them. Then when children become angry, they know what to do to help themselves recover from it.

EXERCISES

Anger

1. How was anger expressed by your parents?

2. How did you feel about parental anger as a child?

3. What situations tend to make you angry as an adult?

4. How do you usually express your anger?

5. Identify three primary feelings that often lead to anger (example: frustration):

6. Identify three physical feelings that occur during your anger response (example: clenched jaw):

7. Think of three positive ways you might use to express anger without hurting yourself or others (example: take a walk):

Dealing with Stress

A person is more irritable and prone to anger when he is under stress. We can define stress as an overload: it might be emotional, mental or physical. The fast pace of life and the growth of complexity in our world affect each one of us, including our children.

The stress response is equivalent to the anger response. When under a significant amount of stress, or when under a sustained (smaller) amount of stress, the body reacts very similarly to the anger response. Adrenaline flows through the system and the body readies itself for fight or flight. Children as well as adults experience the stress response.

| STRESS RESPONSE | ←→ | ANGER RESPONSE | ←→ | FIGHT OR FLIGHT RESPONSE |

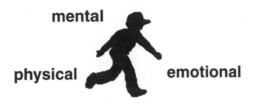

mental

physical   emotional

1. Heart beats faster.
2. Breathing quickens and becomes more shallow.
3. Liver frees stored nutrients for added nourishment.
4. Extra blood carries nutrients to muscles and brain.
5. This emergency delivery raises blood pressure.
6. Digestive system shuts down.
7. Eyes dilate for better vision.
8. Muscles tighten, tense feeling arises, ready to act, to fight or flee.

In addition to stress-management techniques such as relaxation, exercise and listening to music, here are some ways that can help parents put stress into perspective:

1. Be aware of your child's developmental stage. Knowing the stages children go through on their way to adulthood can help parents accept some of the more stressful times. After a stressful period when the child is learning significant developmental steps—such as walking, talking or cognitive changes—there is usually a plateau where things go easier for a while (see the developmental staircase in chapter 1). If your child is going through a difficult stage, chances are a smoother stage will follow.

2. Look through your child's eyes. Whenever you can, put yourself in your child's place. When feeling angry or impatient, try to understand what your child is feeling and why she may have behaved a certain way. Many times we feel our children are being irresponsible when in fact they may just be having an off day, or feeling lively and unable to contain themselves, or needing some positive attention or trying to protect a fragile ego. When we look through our children's eyes, suddenly our adult concerns become less rigid and it is easier to connect with our children's needs.

3. *Analyze what's really bothering you.* If we find ourselves snapping too frequently or too sharply at our children, it may be that adult stress is influencing the way we discipline. Many times stress from the workplace follows us home, or worries about finances sit on our shoulders and color the way we perceive our children's behavior. Perhaps they are doing something they shouldn't be doing—making too much noise or watching television instead of doing their homework. Adult worries and stress can cause a parent to deal much more harshly with a child than the behavior warrants. Choose discipline that fits the child's situation.

4. *Focus on what's going right.* Don't lose appreciation for the wonder of a child. Every child, no matter how difficult his behavior, has positive characteristics. If you can focus on your child's energy and enthusiasm (instead of his perpetual motion or inability to handle frustration), you will have a more positive image of your child, and his image of himself will also be more positive.

5. *Use positive self-talk* and teach your child how to use it. Negative self-talk discourages and defeats. Positive self-talk encourages and overcomes stress. We can memorize some positive statements to keep us going when stressful situations overwhelm us. Teach simple statements to your children—such as "I can do it"—to help them handle stress.

6. *Remember the values you want to teach.* When we choose a discipline technique in advance, we are ready for the child's behavior and much less likely to feel pushed into the use of punishment. But sometimes a child behaves inappropriately when we are not ready for it or when we have no idea what to do about it. In these situations, remember what you most want to teach your child. Do you want him to have a strong positive image of himself? Do you want him to learn

decision-making skills? To get along with others? If you keep in mind the values you most want him to learn, you will handle the situation more appropriately than if you react blindly.

7. *Actively problem-solve.* Involve children in solving problems— not only their problems, but your own small problems as well. (Avoid too-serious problems that are actually adult decisions and would put too large a burden on children's shoulders.) Lead them verbally through the problem-solving process so they can hear the steps that are required. Ask them for their ideas. "Aunt Linda is coming to visit. What activities do you think she might like?" "Grandma's birthday is tomorrow and I forgot to mail her card in time. What do you think we could do about it?" "The library doesn't have any books about Jessica's research report. How can she find some information on state parks?"

8. *Distract yourself (and your children) with pleasant thoughts.* Sometimes the stress piles up or an incident happens that is simply unpleasant and there is nothing you can do about it. This is the time to anticipate the hot soak in the bathtub, or to remind your children that it's Friday and they can sleep in tomorrow.

9. *Plan how you will cope with a future situation.* If things don't go your way, plan how you can compensate for what has gone wrong. If you are late to a meeting, instead of sitting fuming at each red traffic light, use the time to plan what you will say or do when you arrive at the meeting. If your child's science project isn't coming along as expected, sit down with her and plot how to change strategy and timing. After a disappointing experience, talk together and decide how you might change things in the future.

10. *Reduce disappointment by finding alternatives.* When you plan the out-of-state vacation and at the last minute have to cancel, plan a shorter or less-expensive trip to reduce the disappointment. When it rains and the picnic has to be canceled, how about a pizza party instead? Choosing alternatives greatly eases disappointment. There are times when we cannot control finances, illness or the weather. Having a backup plan (or coming up with one spontaneously) is a valuable tool, not only for dealing with the stress of disappointment but also for modeling coping skills for our children.

Put Stress in Perspective

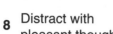
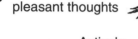

10 Reduce disappointment by finding alternatives

1 Be aware of developmental stages

2 Look through the child's eyes

9 Plan future coping situation

3 Analyze what's really bothering you

8 Distract with pleasant thoughts

4 Focus on what's going right

5 Use positive self-talk

7 Actively problem-solve

6 Remember the values you want to teach

The types of stress that children experience may be different from the stresses we deal with as adults, but the stress response in children is very similar. Stress influences a child's behavior and how he feels about himself. Situations causing major stress for a child include loss of a parent, shared custody between homes, a new child in the family, handicaps and illness, and being retained a year at school. But every day children face smaller stresses that have to be met, from being teased on the playground to skating their best at hockey practice.

Some behaviors tend to indicate that a child is under undue stress, particularly if the child has not shown these behaviors previously: extra dependency, fatigue, nervous habits such as nail-biting or hair-twisting, physical ailments (e.g., constant complaints of tummy aches with no medical basis), escape behaviors such as television-watching, attention-getting behaviors, sleeplessness at night, or strong emotions and moodiness.

Parents and teachers can help children deal with stress by recognizing its widespread influence and by keeping in mind the following coping strategies:

1. Communicate. Take the time to listen to your children's problems, no matter how small. Use the communication techniques outlined in chapters 6 and 7.

Examples of Stress in Children

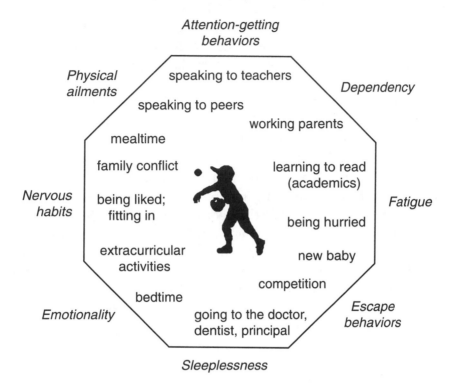

Attention-getting
behaviors

Physical
ailments

speaking to teachers

Dependency

speaking to peers

working parents

mealtime

family conflict

learning to read
(academics)

Nervous
habits

being liked;
fitting in

Fatigue

being hurried

extracurricular
activities

new baby

competition

bedtime

Escape
behaviors

Emotionality

going to the doctor,
dentist, principal

Sleeplessness

The behaviors on the outside of the octagon can be signs of stress overload from the stressors listed on the inside.

2. Be aware of stressors and reduce them, if possible. Realize how constant and troubling the stress of hurrying can be. Anticipate future events to reduce the need for hurrying; plan off-days when no hurrying is required. Prepare children in advance for stressful transitions—particularly the big transitions such as moving between houses in shared custody, going back to school in the fall, going on vacation or moving to a new neighborhood or a new school. Try to find extra patience to help children move through transitions.

3. Have fun together. One of the best antidotes to stress—as well as one of the best ways to build relationships—is to have fun together. Enjoying each other and enjoying life together is one of the rewards of having a family. Humor can defuse potential discipline situations, and it also helps us live longer and enjoy life more.

4. Be in control. Chaos is frightening. Children want to feel confident that an adult is in control and is able to make appropriate decisions. Control does not mean authoritarianism, but rather a flexible, capable leadership role.

5. Reduce competition. One of the strongest avenues of stress for children today is the constant thread of competition that runs through sibling rivalry, scholastic and extracurricular school activities, and even social events. The best antidotes to the stress of competition are encouragement and teaching respect for individual differences. Encourage your child to do his best, regardless of what others are doing around him. There will always be people who perform better than he; there will always be people who perform less well. Accepting this and concentrating on his own performance will encourage a child to do his best while minimizing the stress of the next child's performance.

Encouraging cooperation also minimizes the stress of competition. Despite competition in the business world today, experiments in successful cooperation—such as team decision-making and employee participation in company policy—are increasing. Many schools today are teaching cooperative skills through team projects and study groups. Besides lessening the stress of competition, children learn through cooperative projects that working together can often accomplish more than trying to do it alone.

6. Establish clear, reasonable rules and expectations. Too many rules inhibit a child's creativity and exploration; too few cause anxiety or the feeling that parents don't care. Consistent rules and consequences teach the child responsibility for behavior. Inconsistency often causes the child to believe that he is at fault. If he can break the rule sometimes and it's all right, but at other times it isn't, the child tends to blame himself for being a bad child rather than realizing his actions caused a logical consequence.

Since parents are human, however, it is difficult to be consistent all the time. When a rule needs to be bent or suspended, explain why to the child. "I know that usually it's okay to make noise with your friends, but today I have a headache and would appreciate it if you would play quietly," or "I know you're not allowed to watch television on a school night, but since your homework is finished and I'm working on a big project, it would be all right tonight." Telling your child why the rule has changed helps him understand that outside circumstances have changed it, and not his inner value as a person.

7. *Allow a balance of independence and dependence.* Children want to be connected to the family, but they also want to grow away from it by making individual choices. Allow your child to be independent one minute and then to ask for your strength and reassurance the next minute. Your solid support of your children when they need it will help them grow stronger as they reach out to make their own decisions.

8. *Model creative coping skills.* Every time you model creative problem-solving and healthy anger responses, you are teaching your children how to cope with stress.

What Adults Can Do About Stress in Children

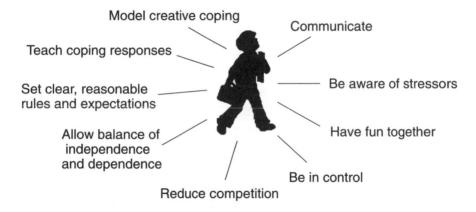

Model creative coping

Teach coping responses

Set clear, reasonable rules and expectations

Allow balance of independence and dependence

Reduce competition

Communicate

Be aware of stressors

Have fun together

Be in control

Stress and anger will continue to be challenges for parents. Having patience with ourselves and not giving up will help us meet these challenges. When we model healthy responses, we are helping our children deal with anger and stress, too.

Chapter 12

Change

Changing Your Discipline Style

New information, especially when it applies to learning a new skill, frequently causes a person to feel anxious. The anxiety includes worry about the old way of doing it, as well as worry about learning and practicing new behaviors. The process of change occurs through six steps:

1. the status quo (the way it used to be),
2. the catalyst, or new information,
3. anxiety,
4. practice,
5. the new skills work with effort, and
6. the new skills work automatically and are incorporated into the style of the learner.

Think back to when you learned how to drive a car. You probably went through the same six stages of change. The status quo was when you didn't know how to drive. Then you took lessons from a driving instructor or from your parents, studying for your beginner's permit and receiving feedback from the instructor as you began to drive. You probably experienced a period of anxiety. Will I be able to do this? What if I do something wrong? Some of the information you learned may have contradicted your earlier perceptions of how to drive correctly.

But with encouragement from your instructor, you began to practice the new driving skills. At first it felt awkward, and every move had to be thought out in advance and consciously executed. But then it became more comfortable, and—as long as you consciously kept track of what you were doing—your driving skills improved and felt more natural. Today your driving skills are second nature; you hardly think about them unless road conditions demand extra attention. You have incorporated driving a car into your style of living.

Changing your discipline style works in a parallel manner. The status quo is whatever you were doing before you read this book. The new information in this book acts as a catalyst and invites you to learn and practice new parenting skills.

It is natural to feel anxious about your past parenting skills or about practicing new skills. It is best to let go of the past; it's over, anyway, and there's not much we can do about it. Abraham Maslow once said that despite the mistakes parents make in bringing up their children, if we love them sincerely, they will probably be all right. What we *can* do is look toward the future and plan to encourage our children, to help them gain confidence and the skills of decision-making, problem-solving and self-discipline.

The next step is to practice the skills you have gained in this book. It is probably helpful at first to choose one or two discipline techniques, and to work for change a little at a time. Breaking hard tasks into steps (just as we do for our children) will encourage success. If appropriate, tell your children (and any other involved adults, such as a noncustodial parent, a babysitter or a teacher) about your desire and suggestions for change. If possible, incorporate their input into your plans.

Don't give up. At first it does take effort, just as it takes effort to learn how to drive a car. Help yourself by putting reminder notes on the refrigerator and taking some time each week to consider how things are going (and preferably to confer with another interested adult). Don't be too hard on yourself if you backslide; new techniques take a while to learn, and parenting—even at its best—is a demanding job.

Enjoy the rewards as the new techniques become part of your style. Many prevention and communication techniques require more energy and time from the parent *at first.* But as children take on more and more responsibility for their actions, discipline becomes easier and easier. For example, when teaching preschoolers how to problem-solve, expect to do a lot of explaining, reminding and practicing with them. But as they grow into school-age children and teens, problem-solving becomes one of the skills they practice every day—and *your* role of disciplining is greatly lightened. In addition, you are giving your children the most valuable gifts that parents can give: positive self-image, the ability to make sound decisions, the skill of problem-solving, and positive relationships with their parents. With these gifts, your children will not only survive the turbulent teen years, but they will have skills that will be useful throughout their lives.

Stages of Change

1. Status quo
2. New information
3. Anxiety
4. Practice
5. Works with effort
6. Works automatically; is incorporated into your style

EXERCISES

Change

1. Choose one technique from the discipline gradient that you would like to try in your family. Why did you choose this technique? With which child(ren) will you try it?

2. With what behaviors would you like to use this technique?

3. How do you think your child will respond to this technique?

4. How will you describe the change to your child? To others?

5. Try the technique. What happened?

6. What did you learn from trying this technique?

7. Will you try the technique any differently the next time? (If so, how?)

A behavioral formula for making change

If you are planning to use a behavior management technique, or if you would like to try a more systematic approach, you may want to try the exercise that follows.

Making Change

1. Identify the behavior you want to change.
2. Set a goal—what is the desirable behavior?
3. Decide how you will go about achieving that goal.
4. Decide consequences.
5. Set a time frame—a starting and an ending date.
6. Communicate the plan to spouse, child and caregivers.
7. Reduce current discipline or punishment.
8. Stay committed to task once you start.
9. Evaluate progress after one, two, three and four weeks.
10. Don't expect perfection—look for improvement in behavior.

If it's not working, change the approach, but communicate the change to everyone involved and be sure you have given it a fair trial first.

EXERCISES

Change—Behavioral Focus

Choose one behavioral problem to work on.

1. Describe the undesirable behavior so it can be observed and measured:

2. What is the desirable behavior you wish to replace it with?

3. What technique(s) will you try to modify your child's behavior?

Change—Behavioral Focus

4. Plan out the strategy you will use. What are rewards, consequences, etc.?

5. When will this plan begin and end?

6. How will you communicate this plan to your child?

7. Who else needs to be told (spouse, teacher, sibling, babysitter)? How will you explain it to them?

8. What current discipline or punishment do you use for this problem?

9. For how long (time period) can you reduce the current discipline to provide a breather before you start the new program?

10. How long will you try this new program?

11. Who can you talk to if you get discouraged?

12. Are you committed to trying this plan for this length of time?

13. How often will you evaluate progress? On what dates?

14. Can you accept improvement instead of perfection?

Sample Answers to Practical Exercises

Chapter 4

Building positive relationships, page 56

1. Hug her, thank her for coming to you, indicate that you will be with her as she faces decisions.

2. Hug him, exclaim with pleasure, go out to dinner to celebrate.

3. Talk to her individually, explain that the class can be difficult, offer individual help.

4. Put on your outdoor clothes and go out to see it, dance a jig together.

5. Do not call attention to times when his voice breaks; when alone, invite him to talk about it, and share growing-up experiences that were hard for you.

Kristi could: involve the children in household chores (ask a different child each evening to help make dinner), tape the television show and watch it after the children are in bed, have lunch with Sally at her day-care center once or twice during the week, take one child along when shopping, take an hour out of a Saturday to spend with one child alone (taking turns), pick up Louis from soccer after work (having time to talk in the car), read some of the books Zachary reads (to be able to talk about them with him), consider negotiating with the children's father so that one child at a time could spend personal time with Kristi, and also with Dad.

Preparing children for events, page 62

Birthday party: Discuss what events will probably happen, act it out, tell a story about a birthday party, let the dolls or bears have a party.

Plane ride: Visit an airport in advance, read a book about airplanes, pretend the kitchen chairs are airplane seats, watch a positive movie about a plane trip.

First time overnight: Choose a teddy bear or other "lovey" to take along, explain about different routines and different food, talk about planned activities, show confidence she'll have a good time but indicate you'll be only a phone call away.

First date: Be open to communication, share date experiences of your own, make clear expectations about rides and curfews, be understanding about nervousness, provide opportunities for teen to talk to friends.

Transition to home: **Warn child it will be time to leave in 15 minutes,** suggest activities to do when you return home.

Transition to bed: Use a routine that includes dressing, tooth-brushing, story-reading.

Transition to school: Allow enough time, choose clothing the night before, have books and lunch ready, outline breakfast options, set up a time schedule for when breakfast should be over and when child should be ready.

Transition to dad's house: Involve child in packing clothing and other supplies, give child a schedule or calendar of where mom will be during the summer, talk about activities the child may be doing with dad, explain transportation schedule, give a small gift to take along (such as a book to read during the summer).

Restructuring time, page 66

Witter family: Provide healthy snacks in advance for Sean's return from school, feed Jesse a little earlier or give him his nap a little later in the afternoon, fix and freeze dinners on weekends for use during the week or have fast-food dinners twice weekly, get Dad involved in making dinner or playing with the kids, suggest that Dad take a few moments to read the paper before he leaves work.

Reducing boredom, page 70

1. Take toys along that are saved for special times, take books to read to Melodie, take snacks.

2. Allow Carol to invite a friend along on the trip, bring along books, encourage her to write a journal or experiment with photography.

3. Allow Timmy to play with fabric scraps, put on children's music or recorded stories to listen to as mother works.

4. Pack a surprise bag of small, inexpensive toys that can be opened periodically, provide headsets with children's stories or music.

5. Allow Janet to bring a doll or stuffed toy to explain things to, pack a small backpack with toys or books, provide a spot at a convenient time for a short nap.

6. Involve the girls in choosing several activities to attend during the day or week—art lessons, swimming, sports, music (join a carpool or help them figure out the bus schedule); help the girls make lists of activities—both household chores and fun activities—that they can

do each day; see if neighbors might have small jobs or babysitting for them to do.

7. Pack a backpack of fun activities for Steven to do while waiting, including art activities and a headset for music or stories.

8. Bring toys, a headset and snacks; consider a children's sewing set for Demetri; check into a shared child-care situation during the weekly meeting.

Changing the environment, page 75

1. Put the cat outside or in another room.

2. Provide a stool so Jerry can reach the faucet, or give him a small pitcher to use if the faucet is too hard to turn.

3. Put out cereal and bowls the night before and allow the children to get their own breakfast.

4. Move the television or the stereo to another room, or provide headphones for Gary.

5. Put the sister's art supplies on a high shelf and create a small store of art supplies for Jack on the lower shelf.

Chapter 5

Substitution, page 79

1. Give Jenny a cloth or plastic book to look at or an old magazine to rip.

2. Guide Corey into the playroom to stack blocks or other appropriate toys on a small table or the floor.

3. Buy Sam a toddler sewing activity (e.g., shoestrings to be threaded into holes punched into cardboard figures). Save this activity for the times when Mom sews.

4. Give Liana her own calendar to mark.

5. Stop at the children's library, the bowling alley or the roller-skating rink.

6. Substitute a children's play or movie; consider visiting musician friends and holding a mini-concert.

7. Substitute another relative to go biking with the children, plan a drive into the country with a picnic, or take the children to a public swimming pool.

Choices, page 86

1. "Would you like to put on your coat first or your boots first?" Or, "Would you like me to help you with your coat or would you like to put it on yourself?"

2. "We have to help clean up in ten minutes. You have time for one more activity. Would you like to finish the board game or try out the cars?" Or, "It is time to go now. When we get home, would you like to eat lunch right away or watch Sesame Street first?"

3. "Would you like to put the plates on the table first or the silverware?" Or, "Would you like to use the white napkins or the green napkins?" Or, "Would you like to wash off the table or would you like me to do that part?"

4. "Do you want to do your math first or work on your social studies project?" Or, "Do you want to work in your room or at the kitchen table?" Or, "Would you like me to work nearby, so you can ask me questions, or would you rather work alone?"

5. "You may eat the food on the table and have dessert, or you may put your dinner in the refrigerator in case you get hungry later, and leave the table" (no other snacks tonight). (If you know your child particularly dislikes a certain food, you could plan several foods that evening and allow him to meet his dessert requirement in a different fashion.)

6. "You can play nicely with Jennie or she can go home now." Or, "If you don't play nicely with Jennie this afternoon, you won't be able to go to her house tomorrow."

7. "You may choose to sit quietly next to me and read your book, or you can go into your bedroom and play while I visit."

8. "You may choose to be on time for curfew or choose to stay home next Friday night." Or, "Car privileges are connected to coming home on time."

9. "You may ride quietly with me in the grocery cart (no sweets), or you may sit in the car with Mom while I shop."

10. "You can make your lunch in the morning or use your allowance to buy hot lunch." Or, "You may make your own lunch in the morning, or I will make it for you if you do another chore for me."

Natural consequences, page 92

1. The child gets burned.

2. The child goes hungry that night.

3. The child is tired for school the next day.

4. The child's siblings won't play with her.

5. The sister hits him back.

6. The teacher catches the student and gives her a zero score.

7. The friend is angry and stops being a friend.

8. The clothes are wrinkled when she wants to wear them again.

9. The teen is not called for future babysitting jobs at that house.

10. The teen doesn't have money for other things she wants or needs (such as the weekend movie with her friends, or special clothes for school).

Chapter 6

Active listening, page 105

Child statements:

1. (Door opener: "What did she do?") Active listening: "Sounds like you and your sister had an argument."

2. (Door opener: "What happened?") Active listening: "I hear you saying Miss Smith doesn't like you for some reason."

3. (Door opener: "What's up, honey?") Active listening: "It's tough to go to school by yourself the very first week."

4. (Door opener: "Wow!") Active listening: "That's wonderful! It takes a lot of work to make the team! I'll bet you feel great!"

5. (Door opener: "Oh?") Active listening: "Sounds like maybe you're missing Mom during preschool."

6. (Door opener: "Why?") Active listening: "You feel upset because he took your toys again."

7. (Door opener: "Uh-huh.") Active listening: "You feel a little lonely with no one to play with."

Teen statements:

1. "A person wants to dress just right for a special party."

2. "You're feeling left out of the group at school."

3. "It's hard to know whether or not to accept a date, even to the prom."

4. "I hear you saying that your project didn't turn out the way you wanted it to."

5. "Sounds like you'd like the car more often."

"I messages," page 117

1. "When you forget to bring your gym shoes to school, I feel frustrated because I don't always have time to drop them off."

2. "When one family member talks on the phone for a long time, I feel concerned that I might be missing some of my calls."

3. "I'm feeling frustrated because the game is so loud I can't hear my friends."

4. "When the cat box doesn't get cleaned, I feel upset because I want the house to be clean for my company."

5. "When you come home late for curfew, I'm very afraid that something might have happened to you."

6. "When you climb on the furniture, I'm worried you might get hurt."

7. "I'm delighted when you pick up your clothes, Laura. It makes my job so much easier."

8. "When you pull on my skirt, I feel frustrated because I can't get the table ready for dinner."

9. "When you tease the cat, I feel anxious because I'm afraid the cat will get angry and you will get hurt."

10. "I feel concerned when I see you watch so much television, because you're not getting your homework done."

11. "When some of the plates are not completely clean, I feel frustrated because I have to go back and redo them."

Chapter 7

Creative problem-solving, page 128

1. Mom and Dad have given their sons an open choice, but when the sons come up with ideas, they are not appropriate (they cost too much). This discourages the boys from the decision-making process, since their input is ignored. It would be better for Mom and Dad to give their children a limited choice—allow their sons to choose between two or three options that are within the family's price range.

2. Bobby's suggestion should not have been ignored, even if it was impractical. (His suggestion might have been molded into a practical one, with other input.) Perhaps Bobby consistently forgot to walk the dog because he had no input in the decision-making. It would be better to write down Bobby's suggestion and include him in the decision-making process, even if he is still young. Other family members might make a commitment to remind him to walk the dog on Tuesdays, or they might even walk with him.

3. The most important thing is to define the situation more clearly. What is being serious? What is being silly? Mother and Joe need to define specifically what should be changed. Should Joe pay closer attention when mother gives him instructions? Should he be more careful to complete chores? Should he giggle less during homework?

Family meetings, page 137

1. Robert's Rules of Order appear to be too complicated for the children to participate freely. It would be better to simplify the rules and obtain better participation and communication.

2. It would be better to make decisions using consensus, rather than majority rule, in the Green family meetings. Then Amanda would no longer find herself in the minority. Meeting leaders could be extra sensitive to Amanda's quietness by asking her questions and patiently waiting until she is able to phrase her thoughts.

3. Family meetings work better when scheduled at a time all members can attend without conflicts. If there are two teenage boys in this family, it might be better to stay away from Friday night scheduling. Positive decisions might be brought up to offset the problems and complaints during meetings. Sally's complaint about the baby could be approached by Sally and her parents outside of the meetings, since the problem has not yet been resolved within the meetings, and since

it concerns only a small part of the family. If Sally is consistently ignored in family meetings, she will lose enthusiasm for the problem-solving process.

Chapter 8

Logical consequences, page 146

1. The child is not allowed in the kitchen until the cooking is done.

2. The child must clean her room before she can invite a friend over to play in the room.

3. The dog is given to a new home. Or, the child must do extra chores for mom, who has taken time to walk the dog.

4. The teen must stay home the next evening he has planned to go out.

5. The child must stay in a separate room from his sister for a period of time.

6. The child must return the merchandise, apologize to the merchant, and volunteer to help the merchant for one weekend.

7. The child must walk to school. Or, the child must do extra chores for dad, who uses his time to drive the child. Or, the child might pay gas money to dad.

8. The teen buys mom a new scarf.

9. The child cannot play outdoors until the school clothes are changed, to prevent wear and tear on the clothes.

10. The child must skip the next opportunity to bake.

Positive reinforcement, page 159

1. The task was too big and should have been broken into steps. It would be better if Rachel earned a sticker for getting her clothes on (or brushing her teeth, or finishing her breakfast). In other words, reward Rachel for one step of getting ready for preschool. When she has accomplished that step, go on to another. Or, allow her to earn three stickers each morning (one for each step), and require about 8 stickers to receive the reward (leaving plenty of room for mistakes).

2. The behavior and the reward were defined too generally. Which chores should Lauren do, and how often do they need to be com-

pleted? What is the surprise (and does Lauren really want it?). Define behaviors and rewards specifically.

3. The parent was accidently reinforcing the undesirable behavior. By giving Jimmy a stick of gum to *stop* misbehaving, Jimmy has learned what to do to receive a stick of gum (be loud in church). Instead, mother should tell Jimmy *before* the service that he may have a stick of gum after church (or toward the end of the service) if he is quiet.

4. The task needs to be defined specifically. Does Shane need to get As to get a television for his room? Or are Cs good enough? Will one quarter's grades be sufficient, or are two quarters required? What if he gets all As and one C? How long can he keep the television? What if his grades fall again? These questions need to be answered before Shane brings home his grades.

5. A family movie is probably not the best motivator for a fifteen-year-old teen, who might be happier seeing a movie with her friends. Allow Sarah to help choose the reward. Also, helping with the dishes every night for two weeks is probably unrealistic: what about extracurricular activities or studying for an unexpected test? Set up the situation so that Sarah will succeed and get the reward. It would be better to ask Sarah to help with dishes for five nights per week, or ten out of fourteen days.

6. Next summer is too far away for a nine-year-old child. Shannon needs something now to reward her for breaking a difficult habit. And, is the reward appropriate for the child? Only if Shannon really wants her room redecorated, and if Mom and Dad can afford it. Involve Shannon in the choice of reward.

Praise, page 165

1. The response links praise with a negative comment, which negates the effect of the praise. It would be better to say only, "I'm glad you washed your hands."

2. The praise could be more specific. "I like the shapes and the way the colors mix together" tells Cheryl that the person has really looked at and enjoyed her picture. It also points out qualities that she can duplicate or expand on in the future.

3. Elizabeth needs encouragement, not praise coupled to an event a whole week ago. A better response would be, "It takes a lot of courage and persistence to learn to swim. I have confidence in you."

4. Randall might suspect the compliment is insincere. Rather than complimenting a bunch of worms with an insincere adjective, a parent might comment on some other aspect: "My, what wiggly worms you found!" or "How long and crawly they are!"

5. Comparison between siblings is a self-esteem crusher. It also provokes competition (and often dislike) between siblings. Although it is difficult sometimes *not* to think of how another child is superior, it is best to avoid comparisons. Instead, respond to the individual child: "I'm glad you're working hard at school. Keep up the good work."

6. It would be even better to tell Brett specifically about his work: "I appreciate the way you never forget to take out the garbage at night, and I particularly like the way you line the baskets with new liners and put them back in place."

7. The compliment to Jackson has a sting to it, even if it might be considered humorous. Teens in particular are hypersensitive about the way they look. It would be better to offer a simple compliment: "I really like your haircut. It looks very attractive."

8. Rather than labeling Carol as a peacemaker (a role she may try too hard to live up to, if she hears it frequently), it would be better to specifically describe her actions. "Thank you for helping your sisters solve their conflict. You stayed calm and offered good advice."

9. At only three years old, Jimmy needs immediate reinforcement. Two days is too long to wait. If the parent wants to reinforce his putting on his pajamas without prompting, she should wait until he does it again, then offer praise immediately.

10. Even though Janell is only four years old, she probably knows it's not the best job of bed-making. If the parent praises her too strongly for a job she feels is barely adequate, Janell might be suspicious of other praise in the future. It would be better to use encouragement (or find a small truth to praise): "Making a bed is not an easy task. I'm delighted you put all the covers back on by yourself." Or, "I like the way you lined up the teddy bears on top."

Star charts and token economies, page 172

For Aaron:

	Mon.	Tues.	Wed.	Thurs.	Fri.
Keeping books in your room neat	★				
Brushing teeth at night	★				
Putting on pajamas at night	★				
Staying in bed					

3 stars/day = 1 extra story at night.
17 stars/week = Aaron picks out a book at the used book store.
Bonus: 4 or more stars on the last row (staying in bed) = can stay up an extra hour on Saturday night.

Or, if the above chart is too hard for Aaron, a simpler chart concentrating on one aspect—such as staying in bed after being tucked in—could be tried.

For Jasmine, Carla, Peter and Kim:

Mrs. Cane can put an empty jar on her desk and add marbles to it whenever the children play together cooperatively. It would be good to have many opportunities per day to add marbles for cooperation, so the jar does not take too long to fill. When the jar is halfway full (to a line marked by a permanent marker), the children will receive an additional trip to the library. When the jar is full, Mrs. Cane will make a pizza party. (Subsequent rewards might be a popcorn party or walking to a pizza parlor.)

Planned ignoring, page 178

1. This situation is not a good choice for planned ignoring because it contains a safety issue (Kristin falling from the furniture).

2. Cameron's mother is actually reinforcing his whining because she occasionally gives in (negative attention when she lectured; positive

attention when she gave him the cookie). Occasional (intermittent) reinforcement is the strongest type.

Cameron's mother might try leaving the room when her son whines (in order not to break down and give him attention). If she cannot ignore him completely, she should choose a different discipline technique.

3.   Although Dad is completely ignoring his son during the church service, Christopher is receiving reinforcement from another source: the two girls in the row behind him who giggle at him. Dad will need to choose another discipline technique (or sit in another location).

4.   This behavior does not seem appropriate for ignoring, since it will influence Jim's schoolwork, grades, and in the long term, possibly even his career. It is unlikely Jim will develop intrinsic motivation to finish homework without adult encouragement, since it is easier to play or watch television than to do homework.

5.   Pam's tattling was reinforced at dinner when Brianna was scolded. (Also, if what Pam said about Brianna was important enough to follow up on, perhaps it was okay for Pam to tell Mom.)

Chapter 9

Contracts, page 187

1.   There is no room for error. It is likely Corey will have a hard time being successful if he is required to meet his goal every night for a period of one month. It would be better to require 18 out of a possible 22 weeknights of doing homework, giving Corey the chance of success even if he has a less-than-perfect score.

2.   "Behaving better in the evenings" is not specific enough for a targeted behavior. It is too difficult to measure, and too difficult for Andy to know what to do to change. Andy and his parents need to define specifically what could be changed about his behavior.

3.   June is receiving reinforcement from sources other than home (the fun of eating sweets with friends). This additional factor needs to be addressed.

4. This is a consequence, not a contract. Contracts are negotiated by both parents and child, and contracts provide a reward or incentive for certain behaviors. (Contracts may also include a consequence, such as not being able to go out the following night.)

5. David may not be sure about the reward. David's parents should include him in the selection process.

Time out, page 194

Mother is angry when she asks Crystal to take a time out, and thus time out becomes a punishment, not a consequence. Mother argues with Crystal while putting her in the time out. Mark interrupts Crystal's time out with impunity. Mother asks Crystal, who is five years old, to stay in a time out for ten minutes (rather than five minutes), but then allows Crystal to come out early. Crystal whines during the time out, and Mother considers the time spent whining as part of the total time out. Mother does not positively reinforce Crystal after the time out (when Crystal engages in positive behavior).

Time out variation, page 198

Mother could create an attractive time-out corner which has books and cassette tapes to listen to. Crystal would be encouraged to enter this corner whenever she began to tease her brother. When Crystal is in the time-out corner, Mark would not be allowed to approach her, nor would Crystal be allowed to speak to Mark. (Mother would have to be vigilant, especially at first.) Crystal could return from the corner whenever she wanted, with the understanding that teasing her brother was not allowed. Mark could also have access to the time-out corner, and Crystal could not talk to him then.

Unrelated consequences, page 202

Logical versus unrelated:
1. unrelated
2. logical
3. logical
4. unrelated
5. logical
6. unrelated

Unrelated consequences:

1. The seven-year-old cannot visit his friend on the weekend.

2. The four-year-old is not allowed to watch television that night.

3. The fourteen-year-old has extra chores to do that night.

Grandma's rule and the broken record, page 208

1. "You may watch television after you make your bed."

2. "You may ride your bike after your daily chores are done."

3. "You may have a cookie as soon as you sit on the potty for a few minutes."

4. Con 2. "You may go to the party after you take your brother to his piano lesson."

5. Con 2. "I'll read you a story as soon as you put on your pajamas."

6. Con 1. "You may have dessert as soon as you have finished your dinner."

7. Con 1. "We will go to the store as soon as you pick up your toys."

8. Con 3. "Your friend can come over as soon as you change your clothes."

9. Con 2. "You may go to the library after this week's chores are finished."

Grounding, page 213

Many possibilities exist for the five situations described. Here are some examples:

1. Two (or possibly three) weeks' loss of weekend *and* weekday social activities with friends (family privileges and phone privileges remain).

2. One week's loss of weekend *and* weekday social activities with friends (family privileges and phone privileges remain).

3. The next weekend's loss of social activities with friends (all other privileges remain).

4. Two weeks' loss of weekday social privileges with friends—no visiting girlfriends' homes after school (all other privileges remain).

5. One (or two) weekends' loss of social privileges with friends (all other privileges remain).

Chapter 10

Punishment, page 221

1. Amanda's mother used punishment because she scolded and threatened Amanda, and the lengthy time out (the entire afternoon) was an unreasonable consequence for a three-year-old. Anticipation techniques (such as locking the door to the study) would have prevented Amanda from reaching the computer.

2. David's mother used punishment because she used scolding and spanking. Anticipation techniques might include mother giving David a nap before the shopping trip. It is difficult for a tired two-year-old toddler to successfully complete a shopping session.

3. Spanking is on the punishment end of the gradient. A month's grounding seems excessive. A more effective way to deal with the situation is to require Shawna to return the necklace to her friend, and to apologize to her friend and her friend's parents (logical consequences).

4. Slapping is physically hurtful. The threat "or else" seems implied when Dad told her not to sass back. Both of these are punishment. Both cause pain and resentment. It would be more effective to use logical consequences, creative problem-solving or a contract.

5. Two months' grounding with no privileges is a very large punishment. Its excessiveness may cause Joel to feel resentment and skip class again to spite his parents. It would be better to try a behavioral contract or a smaller, less restrictive grounding session along with the use of communication techniques.

References and Further Reading

Chapter 1

Turecki, Stanley. *The Difficult Child*. New York: Bantam, 1985.

Maslow, Abraham. *Motivation and Personality*. New York: Harper, 1970.

Berger, Kathleen Stassen. *The Developing Person*. New York: Worth Publishers, 1980.

Elkind, David. *All Grown Up and No Place to Go*. Reading, Massachusetts: Addison-Wesley, 1984.

Chapter 2

Briggs, Dorothy Corkille. *Your Child's Self-Esteem*. Garden City, New York: Doubleday, 1975.

Chapter 4

Brazelton, T. Berry. *Families: Crisis and Caring*. New York: Ballantine, 1989.

Sanger, Sirgay, and Kelly, John. *The Woman Who Works, The Parent Who Cares*. Boston: Little, Brown, 1987.

Chapter 5

Ansbacher, H.L., and Ansbacher, R.R. (Eds.). *The Individual Psychology of Alfred Adler*. New York: Basic Books, 1956.

Dreikurs, Rudolf, and Soltz, Vicki. *Children: The Challenge*. New York: Hawthorn, 1964.

Chapter 6

Rodgers, Carl. *On Becoming a Person*. Boston: Houghton Mifflin, 1961.

Gordon, Thomas. *P.E.T.: Parent Effectiveness Training*. New York: New American Library, 1975.

Chapter 7

Gordon, Thomas. *P.E.T.: Parent Effectiveness Training*. New York: New American Library, 1975.

Dodson, Fitzhugh. *How to Discipline With Love*. New York: New American Library, 1978.

Davis, Gary. *Psychology of Problem Solving*. New York: Basic Books, 1973.

Dreikurs, Rudolf, and Soltz, Vicki. *Children: The Challenge.* New York: Hawthorn, 1964.

Grey, Loren. *Discipline Without Fear.* New York: Hawthorn, 1974.

Painter, Genevieve, and Corsini, Raymond. *The Practical Parent.* New York: Simon & Schuster, 1984.

Chapter 8

Dreikurs, Rudolf, and Soltz, Vicki. *Children: The Challenge.* New York: Hawthorn, 1964.

Dodson, Fitzhugh. *How to Discipline With Love.* New York: New American Library, 1978.

Popkin, Michael. *Active Parenting.* San Francisco: Harper & Row, 1987.

Rachlin, Howard. *Introduction to Modern Behaviorism.* San Francisco: W. H. Freeman, 1970.

Chapter 9

DeRisi, William, and Butz, George. *Writing Behavioral Contracts.* Champaign, Illinois: Research Press, 1975.

Nelsen, Jane, and Glenn, H. Stephen. *Time Out: Abuses and Effective Uses.* Provo, Utah: Sunrise Books, 1991.

Becker, Wesley. *Parents Are Teachers.* Champaign, Illinois: Research Press, 1971.

Coloroso, Barbara. *Discipline: Kids Are Worth It.* New York: Avon, 1994.

Chapter 11

Tavris, Carol. *Anger: The Misunderstood Emotion.* New York: Simon & Schuster, 1989.

Naki, Barbara. "Cycle of Anger." Unpublished presentation. Honolulu, Hawaii, 1975.

Further Reading

Clarke, Jean Illsley. *Self-Esteem: A Family Affair.* Minneapolis: Winston Press, 1978.

Faber, Adele, and Mazlish, Elaine. *How To Talk So Kids Will Listen and Listen So Kids Will Talk.* New York: Avon, 1980.

Faber, Adele, and Mazlish, Elaine. *Siblings Without Rivalry.* New York: Avon, 1987.

Glenn, H. Stephen, and Nelsen, Jane. *Raising Self-Reliant Children in a Self-Indulgent World.* Rocklin, California: Prima Publishing & Communications, 1989.

Index

Praise 161–165
    exercises 165–167
Preparing children for events 59–61
Preschoolers 20–22
    and boredom 67–68
    and egocentricity 22
    and imaginary friends 21–22
    and initiative 20
    and nightmares 21–22
    and self-esteem 20–21
    and symbolic thinking 21
Prevention techniques 43, 49
Problem-solving
    and anger 229–230
Problem-solving, creative 121–128
    exercises 128–130
    with young children 126–128
Punishment 200–201, 215–221
    definition 215–216
    difference between discipline and
        219
    disadvantages 217–219
    exercises 221–223
Punishment techniques 44

Quality time 54, 55

Reading 31
Reinforcement, positive. *See* Positive
    reinforcement
Relationship, parent-child 48, 52, 54, 55
    and modeling 28
    building positive 7–8
    with a strong-willed child 7–8
Relationships
    building 49–55
    exercises 56–57
Responsibility 90, 142, 143
    and choices 83
    and "I messages" 115
    and time outs 191–192
    teaching 65
    teaching a strong-willed child 7
Restructuring time 64–65

Rituals 59–60
Rodgers, Carl 97
Role-playing 12

Sanger, Sirgay 54
School-age children 22–23
    and boredom 68
    and independence 23
    and self-esteem 22
Self-esteem 34–40
    and choices 83
    and communicating acceptance
        51–52
    and criticism 35–36
    and expectations 38–40
    and nurturing 30, 38
    and parent-child relationship 54
    and parenting skills 27, 35
    in infants 18
    in school-age children 22
    influences of 34
    origins 35–36
    in preschoolers 20–21
    reasons for negative 14
    self-reinforcing cycle 14
    two aspects to 37–38
Self-reinforcing cycles 13–14, 34
Shy child
    characteristics of 11
    strategies for 11–13
Skinner, B. F. 139
Sleep problems 45–46
Social learning. *See* Positive
    reinforcement
Spanking 217
Spencer, Herbert 89, 141
Spending time with a child 52–55
Star charts 167–172
    exercises 172–174
Stress 225, 232–239
    in children 40, 236–239
    in normal developmental stages
        24–26

About the Author

Susan Thierman has been involved in parenting education for more than fifteen years. She received her M.Ed. in community counseling and her M.F.A. in creative writing from the University of Alaska Fairbanks, and she is a nationally certified family life educator. Susan lives with her husband and three children in Fairbanks, Alaska.